Mother–Child and Father–Child Psychotherapy

Mother–Child and Father–Child Psychotherapy

A Manual for the Treatment of Relational Disturbances in Childhood

M. Ben-Aaron, J. Harel, H. Kaplan, R. Patt
University of Haifa

With contributions from

D. Glat, E. Raz, A. Wasserman, M. Winer
University of Haifa

Introduction by P. Fonagy and M. Target
University College London

W
WHURR PUBLISHERS
LONDON AND PHILADELPHIA

First published 2001 by
Whurr Publishers Ltd
19b Compton Terrace, London N1 2UN, England and
325 Chestnut Street, Philadelphia PA 1906, USA

British Library Cataloguing in Publication Data
A catalogue record for this book is available from the British Library.

ISBN: 1 86156 180 6

Contents

Contributing authors

Miriam Ben-Aaron Senior Supervising Clinical and Developmental Psychologist, Faculty Post Graduate Program for Psychotherapy Studies, Department of Psychology, University of Haifa. Consultant to Haamakim Clinic, Founder and Past Director Child Psychological Development Clinic, Ministry of Health.

Peter Fonagy Freud Memorial Professor of Psychoanalysis, University College London. Director of Research, The Anna Freud Centre. Director, Child and Family Center and Center for Outcomes Research and Effectiveness, Menninger Foundation.

Dina Glat Clinical Psychologist, Supervising Educational Psychologist, Clinical Tutor Post Graduate Program for Psychotherapy Studies, Department of Psychology, University of Haifa.

Judith Harel Supervising Clinical and Developmental Psychologist, Hanna Khoushy Child Development Center – Bnei-Zion Medical Center, Senior Lecturer Department of Psychology, Faculty Post Graduate Program for Psychotherapy Studies, Department of Psychology, University of Haifa.

Hayuta Kaplan Supervising Clinical Psychologist, Child Psychological Development Clinic, Ministry of Health, Faculty Post Graduate Program for Psychotherapy Studies, Department of Psychology, University of Haifa.

Raya Patt Supervising Clinical and Developmental Psychologist, Child Psychological-Development Clinic, Ministry of Health, Faculty Post Graduate Program for Psychotherapy Studies, Department of Psychology, University of Haifa.

Edna Raz Supervising Social Worker, Hanna Khoushy Child Development Center – Bnei-Zion Medical Center, Lecturer Post Graduate Program for Psychotherapy Studies, Department of Psychology, University of Haifa.

Mary Target Senior Lecturer in Psychoanalysis, University College London, Deputy Director of Research, The Anna Freud Centre.

Ariela Wasserman Clinical Psychologist, Lecturer Post Graduate Program for Psychotherapy Studies, Department of Psychology, University of Haifa.

Michal Winer Clinical Psychologist, Clinical Tutor Post Graduate Program for Psychotherapy Studies, Department of Psychology, University of Haifa.

Acknowledgements

We are very grateful to Mary and Julian Target who edited this English translation of the manual.

The approach presented should be seen as a collaborative effort of many psychotherapists working with children, who feel the need to include the parents – mother and father – as the most significant vehicles of change in the process of helping the child.

The psychotherapists, our co-workers, colleagues and students, working in different clinical set-ups and serving diverse populations, are far too many to be mentioned individually. We thank them all for the many years of thoughtful discussions and fruitful sharing.

Introduction: the historical background of psychoanalytic psychotherapy for children

PETER FONAGY AND MARY TARGET

What is psychodynamic psychotherapy?

Psychodynamic psychotherapy covers a wide range of treatment approaches. These range from child psychoanalysis (Sandler *et al.*, 1980), through once weekly individual therapy (Kernberg, 1995), group implementation (Rose, 1972), family-based implementations (Selvini *et al.*, 1978) and many others. Psychodynamic therapies in themselves differ in terms of the use made of expressive versus supportive techniques (Luborsky, 1984), the emphasis placed on play (Schaefer and Cangelosi, 1993; Simon, 1992) or drama (Johnson, 1982). In addition there are major theoretical divisions which overlap in part with issues of technique originating from different understandings of the nature of development and psychopathology (King and Steiner, 1991).

Psychodynamic approaches, however, share an understanding of psychological abnormality as being a consequence of conflicting motivational states. Such states are often seen to be unconscious and the conflict created seems to be intrapsychic (e.g. Brenner, 1982). It is not invariably the case that approaches emphasizing interpersonal rather than intrapsychic conflicts have been gaining ground in contemporary psychodynamic theorization (Klerman *et al.*, 1984). Psychodynamic treatment is considered to be therapeutic by the assisting of individuals to build on their inherent capacities for understanding and emotional responsiveness. This is facilitated by a therapeutic relationship, and in particular by the therapist's communication of her understanding of the patient's conflicting motivations and responses to these conflicts. (For reasons of simplicity therapists will be referred to generically as 'she' and patients as 'he'.) Via such intervention the patient may be enabled to arrive at more adaptive solutions than the rather limited strategies that brought him to seek psychological help. In this sense mother–child and father–child psychotherapy is a genuinely psychodynamic treatment.

Theoretical frameworks in psychodynamic therapy

Psychodynamic approaches to the treatment of children are based on a heterogeneous set of theories. Freud's original developmental formulations (Freud, 1905) suggest that the child is constitutionally predisposed to an inevitably partially successful struggle to adapt his sexual and aggressive instincts to the demands of a civilized society. Freud (1933) paints a picture of the child as an individual in turmoil, in a constant struggle to master biological needs and make these acceptable to the external world, or rather to society at large. The drama takes place universally in the development of every human being within the microcosm of the family (Freud, 1930).

Over a period of 45 years of psychoanalytic writing, Freud's thinking gradually moved away from a position where he saw psychological problems as arising out of suppressed emotions gaining expression through symptomatology, to an increasingly complex view, where the counterbalance of psychological forces within the mind was seen as the critical aspect of psychological adaptation. In his last full formulation (the so-called 'structural' model) (Freud, 1923) Freud envisioned three psychic agencies: (a) instinctual, principally sexual and aggressive energies located within the *id*; (b) a moral code embedded within the *super ego*; and (c) adaptive mechanisms organized within the *ego*. He elaborated a complex model whereby normal adaptation could be seen as the harmonious functioning of these agencies, whilst psychological abnormality invariably reflected a breakdown of the ego's capacity to respond to the demands of the id, the super ego and the external environment.

American ego psychology, particularly the work of Heinz Hartmann (1939), was highly successful in elaborating the model. Hartmann, and other ego psychologists, were the first to delineate clearly how adverse experiences in early development may jeopardize the development of mental structures essential to adequate adaptation. Ego psychologists were also able to be more specific about how the reactivation of early developmental structures (ego regression) was an important component of most psychopathology (Hartmann, 1955).

Freud's daughter, Anna Freud, was strongly influenced by these psychological ideas of the North American psychoanalytic tradition, although her practice was in London, England. Her major contribution was in linking normal emotional development to diagnosable psychopathology (Freud, 1965). She charted normal development along a series of 'developmental lines' and made the powerful suggestion that equilibrium between developmental processes was a key aspect of normal development. A child whose environment selectively compromised some but not other developmental processes was considered at risk of maladjustment and psychopathology. Her vision of the relationship of development and psychopathology lies, conceptually at least, at the heart of the new, integrative discipline of developmental psychopathology (see for example Sroufe, 1990).

While Anna Freud elaborated her father's work, particularly in the context of the child's relationship to external reality (see for example Goldstein *et al.*, 1973), other psychodynamic thinkers focused on the potentially conflictual aspects of intrapersonal development. Margaret Mahler (1968), for example, drew attention to a paradoxical aspect of self-development. She pointed out that the achievement of an independent identity, upon which Western civilization places such high value, brings with it the sacrifice of a gratifying and intimate relationship with the primary caregiver. She observed that parents varied in their capacity to facilitate the child's achievement of 'individuation'. She suggested that the failure to develop a separate coherent sense of self may be rooted in the caregiver's reaction to the toddler. Rather than supporting the child's independence, the caregiver shows a tendency to withdraw from the child as the child manifests early signs of independence (Masterson, 1972; Rinsley, 1977). The ego psychological model was further elaborated by Edith Jacobson (1964) and Joseph Sandler (1987). Both these theoreticians suggested a move away from the mechanistic psychological model suggested by Freud to a model far more compatible with modern cognitive neuroscience. These models de-emphasize the biologically rooted notions of drives and instincts and replace these with constructs such as wishes and the role of representational structures in the child's mind and how these might mediate both reality and its distortion associated with internal conflict.

In the meantime, in the United Kingdom a completely different approach to psychodynamic theory grew out of the work of Melanie Klein (Klein *et al.*, 1946). One of Melanie Klein's fundamental postulates was the assumption of two radically different modes of mental functioning. The first, ***the paranoid-schizoid position***, described the state of mind (prototypically in the human infant) that was incapable of tolerating simultaneous loving and destructive feelings towards his love object and dealt with the conflict by splitting, that is creating separate images of the loved and the hated figure. With cognitive development, this inevitably leads to what Melanie Klein called *the depressive position*, when the child recognizes that the object he loved and the one he hated are one and the same. Klein's original ideas met with considerable scepticism because of the extravagant assumptions she was ready to make about the cognitive capacities of infants, which were incompatible with the then state of developmental knowledge. More recently developmental research has confirmed many of Klein's claims, for example those concerning the perception of causality (Bower, 1989) and causal reasoning (Golinkoff *et al.*, 1984). Klein's ideas rapidly became popular, principally because of the helpfulness of her clinical observations. For example, she proposed the notion of *projective identification* to account for the common experience of therapists that patients can exert significant influence over their state of mind. Working within a Kleinian framework, a number of psychoanalysts have elaborated ideas on how early emotional conflict may impact on the child's developing cognitive capacities (e.g. Bion, 1962; Rosenfeld, 1971). Klein believed that projection was the most basic mechanism available to children to deal with destructiveness. They struggle to rid themselves of their destructive fantasies by placing them on to other persons. It is only through the therapist's interpretive work, particularly of such destructive fantasies, that children are enabled to reclaim disowned aspects of themselves and allow for the development of a less malevolent and more realistic appraisal of others.

Early development was also the focus of another extremely important strand of psychoanalytic thought – that of the British object relations theorists. Foremost amongst these was Fairbairn (1952) who shifted theoretical emphasis from the satisfaction of biological desires to the individual's need for the other. Working in this tradition, and also influenced by Melanie Klein, Donald Winnicott (1965) proposed a number of fundamental psychodynamic developmental notions such as *primary maternal preoccupation*, the *mirroring* function of the caregiver, and the *transitional space* in development between fusion and separateness within which symbolic thought and play were considered to be rooted. Most recent studies offer support for Winnicott's assertions concerning the traumatic consequences of early maternal failure, particularly maternal depression (see for example Cummings and Davies, 1994).

Probably influenced by the work of Donald Winnicott, Heinz Kohut (1977) rekindled the interest of psychoanalysts in North America in the interpersonal aspects of early development. The caregiver's role is seen as one of mirroring and the goal of development is one of achieving a coherent sense of self. If the caregiver is able to become a 'self-object', empathically attuned to the infant's or young child's mental states, the child's sense of personhood will be firmly established. Within a self-psychology, drive theory took secondary importance. Kohut (1971) suggested that the dominance of drives were themselves indications of the child's failure to have attained an integrated self-structure that would normally regulate drive states adequately. Kohut's formulations concerning narcissistic personality structures have been highly influential and helpful in extending the applicability of psychodynamic approaches from the strictly neurotic to the so-called character disorder spectrum of disorders.

A similar extension of the application of psychodynamic concepts may be attributed to the work of Otto Kernberg (Kernberg, 1976, 1987). Kernberg followed Jacobson and Sandler in seeing the mind as principally a representational organ. He postulated the existence of relationship representations consisting of self, object and affect which characterize the specific relationship. Kernberg reconceptualized the theory of drives, seeing these as developmental achievements, integrations of multiple *triadic self–object–affect representations*. Whilst in neurotic cases the integration achieved is relatively complete, in personality disorder the self and other representations are only partial and infused with overwhelming and extreme emotional states of both ecstasy and persecutory terror and aggression. Kernberg's ideas have been enormously influential in psychoanalytic thinking and are particularly helpful because they lend themselves relatively well to operationalization and empirical study (Clarkin *et al.*, 1999).

Sharing the virtue of openness to empirical scrutiny is John Bowlby's proposal of attachment theory (Bowlby, 1969, 1973, 1980). Bowlby's ideas placed primary emphasis on the earliest relationship within which safety and predictability must be experienced in order for the child to acquire a capacity for relatively problem-free later interpersonal relationships. Bowlby assumes that representational systems, *internal working models*, evolve based on a template created by the earliest relationship of the infant to the caregiver. If the expectancy of need and distress being met by comforting is encoded into these models the child will be able to approach relationships in a relatively undefensive way. If this is not the case, if the child's caregivers lacked sensitivity (Ainsworth *et al.*, 1978), the child's representational system will be defensively distorted so as either to minimize or heighten experiences of arousal, and dismiss or become entangled in the response of others (Main *et al.*, 1985).

Daniel Stern (1985) took a novel approach to the psychoanalytic study of childhood. His description is exceptional in being normative rather than pathomorphic and prospective rather than retrospective. His main concern, as that of Kohut, is the development of a coherent self-structure. His psychoanalytic model, however, has much in common with Sandler's representational theory as well as Kernberg's focus on the affective aspect of early relationships.

As this brief overview of current psychoanalytic models should indicate, there is no agreed-upon formulation that is shared by all psychoanalytic schools. In fact, intense controversy, such as that between Melanie Klein and Anna Freud in the 1940s and 1950s (King and Steiner, 1991), often characterizes psychoanalytic theoretical discussion. Nevertheless, more recently there has been considerable cross-fertilization of ideas and an integrated psychodynamic model may not be too far away (see for example Pine, 1985). There is also an increased emphasis on behavioural research (Emde and Fonagy, 1997) which, in turn, may facilitate the emergence of a core set of psychodynamic theoretical assumptions well supported by empirical data.

Basic assumptions in psychodynamic therapy

Notwithstanding the theoretical heterogeneity of psychoanalytically-based therapeutic approaches, there is probably a core set of assumptions to which all psychodynamic therapists would, to a greater or lesser extent, subscribe. These can be basically summarized as follows:

1. *The notion of psychological causation*. This is not an assumption concerning the psychogenic nature of psychological disturbance, but rather refers to the preferred level of conceptualization for psychodynamic clinicians. Whether psychological problems are genetically or socially determined, psychodynamic therapists assume that the representation of past experience, its interpretation and its meaning, whether conscious or unconscious, determine children's reaction to the external world and their capacity or lack of capacity to adapt to it. This formulation does not imply lack of respect for other levels of analysis of childhood psychological problems, the biological, the sociocultural or the systemic. Rather, psychological difficulties are conceived of as meaningful organizations of a child's conscious or unconscious beliefs, thoughts and feelings and therefore they are assumed to be accessible to psychotherapeutic intervention.
2. *The assumption of unconscious mental processes*. Psychodynamic clinicians assume that the explanation of conscious ideation and intentional behaviour requires the assumption of complex mental processes

functioning outside of awareness. While psychodynamic clinicians probably no longer think in terms of 'an unconscious', in the sense of a physical space where forbidden or repudiated feelings and ideas are stored, they assume that non-conscious fantasies associated with wishes for gratification or safety profoundly influence children's behaviour, their capacity to regulate affect and to handle their social environment adequately.

3. *The assumption of a representational model of the mind.* In common with cognitive scientists, psychodynamic therapists assume that the experience of self with others is internalized, and forms the basis for relatively enduring representational structures of social and interpersonal interactions. These representational structures determine interpersonal expectations and shape the mental representation of the self.
4. *The pathogenic significance of conflict.* Intrapsychic conflict (incompatible wishes, affects or ideas) is assumed to be ubiquitous in development. It is seen as the cause of displeasure as well as an absence of safety. Adverse environments tend to intensify conflicts as well as undermine the development of capacities that may help the child in dealing with conflictual aspects of ordinary life. For example, the loss of a caregiver or severe neglect or abuse may aggravate a natural predisposition to relate with mixed feelings to the caregiver, as well as reducing the child's competence in resolving such incompatible ideas.
5. *The assumption of psychic defences.* It is assumed that children rapidly develop an unconscious capacity to modify unacceptable or dangerous ideas, desires or affects by resorting to a set of mental operations that have in common the function of distorting these mental states in a direction of reducing their capacity to generate anxiety, distress or displeasure. Like all mental operations, defences have a developmental or maturational hierarchy. More complex defences, such as intellectualization or humour, come into effect relatively late in development or perhaps never. Simpler processes such as projection, denial or splitting are available to the child from a relatively early stage.
6. *The assumption of complex meanings.* Psychodynamic therapists assume that children's communication within the treatment context has meanings beyond that intended by the child. Likewise, children's symptoms might carry multiple meanings reflecting the nature of the child's internal representations of himself and others. Within a classical formulation, symptoms express a combination of a wish as well as the child's attempt to erect a defensive, self-protective set of mental operations to protect himself from that wish. The therapist's task is to make

appropriate links between the child's behaviours in different contexts that may show the child that the behaviour that is seemingly bizarre, confusing, frightening or even self-destructive has a meaningful and even rational facet when looked at from a different perspective or in a different context. Elaborating and clarifying such meaning structures may be seen as the essence of psychodynamic psychotherapy.

7. *The assumption of transference displacement*. It is generally accepted that internalized representations of interpersonal relationships which determine the child's behaviour with others in the outside world also become active in the context of the therapeutic relationship. The displacement of patterns of expectation from important others in the child's life to the therapist serves as a window on the child's internal world. This function becomes all the more important because the relative neutrality and ambiguity of the therapeutic relationship encourages externalizations of repudiated aspects of past relationships (Tyson and Tyson, 1986). The situation becomes more complicated since the child's verbal and non-verbal behaviour must naturally have an impact on the therapist's experience. However, modern psychodynamic therapists tend to make extensive use of their subjective reactions to help them understand the roles that they are implicitly asked by the child to play. In this way the therapist is able to gain a view of the child's internal struggles and representations of both himself and others.
8. *The therapeutic aspect of the relationship*. Psychodynamic therapists assume that, in addition to new understanding and insight that the child might gain through the experience of therapy, aspects of the relationship with a supportive and respectful empathic adult will also have benefits for the child's functioning. In particular the therapist's interest in the child's mental states, talk and play, thoughts and feelings, and the therapist's commitment to find meaning even in the disruptive or distressing aspects of the child's behaviour provides him with an opportunity to reflect upon and reorganize experiences and identify more adaptive solutions to the interpersonal and intrapsychic conflicts he faces.

The evolution of psychodynamic child psychotherapy

Freud was an acute observer of the behaviour of young children. He used his observations to support and elaborate his assumptions about infantile mental processes (see for example Freud, 1900, 1909, 1920, 1926).

Although these observations were detailed and accurate he was sceptical about their value in clinical work with psychologically disordered children. It was Hug-Helmuth (1920) who first used the play of children as part of an insight-oriented technique. She saw the child's play in a therapeutic context as providing insight into the child's unconscious sexual fantasies, which could then be interpreted.

The true originators of psychodynamic psychotherapy for children were Anna Freud (1946) and Melanie Klein (1932). They evolved somewhat different, yet in important ways compatible, approaches that enabled psychodynamic clinicians to work with children. Klein's approach was based on the assumption that children's play was essentially the same as the free association of adults. She saw such play as motivated by unconscious fantasies activated principally by specific aspects of the relationship with the therapist. It therefore required interpretation, or at least clarification, if the child's anxiety was to be addressed by the therapist. The principal focus of Klein's therapeutic work was the interpretation of the child's deeply unconscious concerns related to destructive and sadistic impulses. Klein was exclusively concerned with the unconscious aspects of the child's behaviour in the therapeutic setting and had minimal interest in other aspects of the child's life, such as the child's relationship with his parents or other adults.

At the heart of the Kleinian psychotherapeutic technique is the notion of projection. Projection is considered by Klein (1946, 1952) as an unconscious fantasy placing part of the child's self into another person and obtaining a degree of relief from experiencing unwanted feelings as no longer belonging to the self. This leads to a form of fragmentation of the self (the paranoid-schizoid position) which, whilst normal in infancy, may cause significant pathology later in life. The transference is seen by Kleinian therapists as central to interpretive work since it is the unwanted projected aspects of the child's experience of himself that need to be reintegrated in order to achieve therapeutic benefit.

Kleinian technique with children has changed considerably since the early days. Modern Kleinians (e.g. DeFolch, 1988; O'Shaughnessy, 1988) would not often give direct interpretations of deeply unconscious material. Bion (1959) emphasized the importance of 'containment', that is the therapist's capacity to understand and accept the child's projections. This may be critical in normal development (in the caregiver) as well as in the therapist's experience of the countertransference.

Anna Freud's approach was deeply rooted in the developmental context of the child's efforts to achieve a reasonable adaptation to a social and an internal environment. She was reluctant to make assumptions concerning the meaning of the child's play and, in comparison with Melanie Klein, approached the work of interpretation far more gradually. She worked in close collaboration with both parents and teachers. She assumed that changes in the child's environment, brought about by communicating to carers an understanding of the child's problems derived from therapy, might have equal if not greater long-term benefit for the child's functioning. Her emphasis was on conflicts arising from the child's sexual impulses rather than, as was Klein's, on innate aggression. The essential aspect of her technique was the interpretation of the child's strategies of adapting to conflict, the interpretation of defence, and only through this the anxieties which brought them into play. The therapeutic goal is less the achievement of the integration of a fragmented sense of self and object, but rather the developmental goal of returning the child to a normal path of maturation. Consequently she was far more accepting of supportive and educational techniques to address the child's poorly developed ego functions (Pine, 1985).

The third important strand in the development of psychodynamic technique originates in the work of Donald Winnicott (1965, 1971). While influenced by Klein in his model of childhood pathology, his technique, in common with Anna Freud, emphasized the importance of a holding environment as well as the importance of play. Play was seen not simply as a vehicle for communicating unconscious fantasy but as an activity that is uniquely generative of human development. A major contribution of Winnicott is his description of a 'transitional space' between self and object where the subjective object and the truly objective could be simultaneously seen (Winnicott, 1971). This duality of representation created an important bridge between psychodynamic thinking and interpersonalist approaches such as that of Sullivan (1953). Within the interpersonal approach the therapist becomes an active and real participant in the therapeutic situation (Altman, 1992, 1994; Warshaw, 1992).

These trends evolved to some degree independently in different parts of the world. While Kleinian thinking dominated the United Kingdom and, to some degree, Latin America, it was the work of Anna Freud which was most readily integrated into psychodynamic ideas in the United States and some parts of Europe. More recently, interpersonal approaches to psychodynamic therapy have taken hold in many treatment centres in the United States motivated partly by self-psychological Kohutian therapeutic orientation as well as the integration of Winnicottian object-relations approaches. There has also been considerable cross-fertilization of psychoanalytic psychodynamic techniques, even in the more committed Kleinian (e.g. Alvarez, 1993) and Anna Freudian (e.g. Bleiberg *et al.*, 1997) traditions.

The approach described in this volume, mother–child and father–child psychotherapy, takes therapeutic components from each of these orientations. Its novelty lies not in its conceptual roots but rather in the context in which it is administered. By observing, rather than speculating about, the nature of the parent–child relationship the therapist is able to observe the transference (the unconscious attributions of child to parent and parent to child) as it happens rather than infer these structures from the child's reactions to the therapist. This important technical modification makes the treatment more direct, more immediate and, we hope, also more effective. Before reviewing the therapeutic techniques specific to mother–child and father–child psychotherapy it may be helpful to consider briefly the technical features of traditional psychodynamic therapy for children.

The selection of clients for psychodynamic therapy

Traditionally, psychodynamic therapists work with relatively less severely disturbed young people. The criteria of suitability for psychodynamic psychotherapy have been identified by Hoffman (1993), Glenn (1978), Sandler et al. (1980) and others as the following:

1. Good verbal skills and psychological mindedness, that is the ability to conceive of behaviour as mediated by mental states (thoughts and feelings). Equally important here is the child's capacity to tolerate awareness of conflicts and anxieties, particularly those previously kept unconscious, without risking substantial disorganization or disintegration of the personality.
2. A supportive environment which is able to sustain the child's involvement in an intense and demanding long-term interpersonal relationship. Particularly important here is the willingness of parents to respect the boundaries of the child's therapy and promote the child's commitment to the treatment.
3. It is assumed that successful treatment depends on internal conflicts being the cause of the child's disturbance.
4. Further, traditionally psychotherapists were reluctant to treat children with major developmental deficits (ego deviations) which were not the result of unconscious conflict and therefore could not be seen as resolvable through insight.
5. As the child's motivation for treatment stems from anxiety, guilt or other unpleasant affects, these experiences are often seen as essential to ensuring the child's commitment to the treatment as well as a sense of agency (a sense of responsibility for their problems and actions).

6. It is assumed that a capacity to form relationships and develop trust must be present in order for psychodynamic therapy to operate.

The above description corresponds to what has traditionally been referred to as neurotic disturbance. For example, Tyson (1992) describes neurosis as characterized by (a) a predominance of internalized conflicts producing symptoms, (b) a capacity for affect regulation, and (c) a capacity for self-responsibility. Kernberg (1975) has added to this list the predominance of repression as a mechanism of defence. However, neurosis is a term largely discredited in modern descriptive psychiatry as lacking in clarity and reliability and probably also over-inclusive and based on an outmoded theory of psychological disorder. There is evidently a group of children commonly treated by psychodynamic psychotherapy who do not meet the criteria as described above. We have described this group in our retrospective examination of case records at the Anna Freud Centre (Fonagy and Target, 1996a, 1996c). Other descriptions by Cohen *et al.* (1994), Towbin *et al.* (1993) and Bleiberg (1987, 1994a) have arrived at strikingly similar descriptions. This group of children appears to suffer from a variety of deficiencies of psychological capacities, indicated for example by lack of control over affect, lack of stable self and other representations, and diffusion of their sense of identity.

Whereas the two groups may be readily distinguished in terms of descriptive criteria, elsewhere we have tentatively suggested a conceptual framework that may help provide theoretically based psychodynamic distinction (Fonagy *et al.*, 1993). In this model we distinguish children whose problems may be seen as a consequence of distortion in *mental representations*, either of others or of themselves. Such distorted representations may arise out of exceptional environmental factors or defensive distortions associated with various forms of intrapsychic conflict. Broadly speaking, these children correspond to what has traditionally been regarded as the neurotic category. By contrast, children with more severe problems, who usually present with multiple disorders, low levels of adaptation and poor personality functioning, may be seen as suffering from defensive inhibition or distortion of *mental processes* rather than just the mental representations which such processes generate. Thus for this group of children a wide variety of situations is likely to bring about maladaptive functioning, as the very capacities which may be involved in achieving adaptive functioning are impaired. It is important to note that whilst biological factors may play an important role in both types of pathology, in both cases the focus on psychological causation is retained. For example, inhibitions on specific ways of thinking occur as attempts at adaptation.

There are important considerations from the point of view of psychotherapeutic technique that arise out of this distinction. Disorders of mental representation are well served by a primarily interpretive therapeutic process which aims at addressing distorted ideas and integrating repudiated or incoherent notions of self and other. The reintegration of split off (repressed), often infantile but troublesome ideas into the child's developmentally appropriate mental structures is the therapeutic aim (Abrams, 1988). In the more severely disturbed group of patients this kind of approach has limited usefulness. There is a need for strengthening or disinhibiting mental processes which may have been disengaged (decoupled) or distorted for defensive or constitutional biological reasons. These patients may, for example, need assistance in labelling and verbalizing affects and ideas. Much of psychodynamic intervention aimed at the so-called neurotic patient may change the organization or the shape of the child's mental representation (Sandler and Rosenblatt, 1962). To regenerate mental processes an alternative set of psychodynamic techniques, emphasizing a developmental approach, is necessary. Our review of current therapeutic approaches will be based around this distinction.

Therapeutic approaches addressing disorders of mental representation

It follows from the assumptions of psychodynamic psychotherapy reviewed above that child therapists using these techniques expect children to be using distorted and/or unconscious mental representations in maladaptive ways. For example, the child may unconsciously represent his father as cruel and rageful, a representation distorted by the child's unconscious aggression. Further, it is anticipated that these distortions have a developmental dimension whereby ideas or feelings are more appropriate to an earlier stage of development and are likely to confuse the child's current perceptions (Abrams, 1988). The separation (repression, denial, displacement) of such early ideas is assumed to be defensive. For example, the perception of a caregiver as cruel and destructive may be based on an infantile perception of that parent. As a consequence of the pain associated with this perception of a loving father, this representation has never come to be integrated into the evolving representation of the father in the child's mind. It exists as a separate, yet disturbing idea. The child may react to the presence of such a representation as potentially painful and incompatible with his perception of his parent as loving and affectionate. By displacing this perception onto others who he then perceives as frightening he may, for example, exaggerate the subjective likelihood of burglars or other intruders attacking him and his family. Of course, if such ideas are based on the externalization of his own aggressive feelings towards the father then it is these feelings which have to be addressed in the context of the therapy.

The therapist, using the child's verbalization, non-verbal play, dream reports or other behaviours, attempts to create a model of the child's conscious and unconscious thoughts and feelings. On the basis of such a model the therapist assists the child to acquire an understanding of his irrational or at times inappropriate feelings and beliefs. This kind of understanding may, under ideal conditions, result in the integration of developmentally earlier modes of thinking into a more mature and age-appropriate framework. The structure of the treatment appears to be relatively unimportant. Some therapists use toys or games, others more readily engage children in a process of self-exploration. In most contexts the therapist works to draw attention to possible unconscious determinants of the child's behaviour. Therapists tend to use material of the child's fantasy and play in conjunction with other information they have obtained about the child (parental reports, school reports etc.) to construct a plausible picture of the child's emotional concerns. The most common foci of psychodynamic child therapists tend to be the child's concerns about his body, anxieties about conscious or unconscious destructive or sexual impulses, and concerns about relationships with or between caregivers or siblings or peers.

A range of techniques is standardly used by psychodynamic therapists. These have been systematized on the basis of empirical studies by Paulina Kernberg (1995), who observed a number of somewhat overlapping but reliably distinguishable categories of interventions. These include:

1. *supportive interventions* aimed at reducing the child's anxiety or increasing his sense of competence and mastery using suggestion, reassurance, empathy or the provision of information;
2. *summary statements* or paraphrases of the child's communication to that point which support and develop the therapeutic exchange with the child;
3. *clarifications* of the child's verbalization or affect. These help prepare the child for interpretation or simply direct his attention to noticeable aspects of his behaviour such as a repeated tendency to behave in self-defeating, self-destructive ways;
4. *interpretations* attempt to identify and spell out representations which the child is likely not to be aware of and therefore is likely to find diffi-

> cult or totally unacceptable. It is therefore expected that the child will show a certain degree of resistance to such verbalizations on the part of the therapist. Interpretations have to be carefully timed to maximize their acceptability to the child. Ideally the therapist would have accumulated considerable evidence to support her conjectures, making their acceptance more or less automatic.

In formulating an interpretation, the therapist is well advised to concentrate her attention on the therapeutic situation itself, where evidence is most likely to become available. While the therapist may often be able to identify significant connections between the child's behaviour in therapy and what the therapist knows about the child's past experience, interpretations, at least in the early phase of treatment, are best restricted to the child's current conflicts, in the immediate context brought into the therapy. The ultimate aim of the therapist is to provide the child with an emotionally meaningful comprehensive understanding of the connections between past experiences and current methods of coping with conflict.

Kernberg (1995) distinguishes between three kinds of interpretation: (1) interpretations of defence; (2) interpretations addressing repudiated wishes; and (3) reconstructive interpretations. The first of these draws the child's attention to actual exclusion of certain ideas from awareness. This focuses attention on certain contents but also invites the child to consider alternative strategies for coping with or expressing these ideas or feelings. The second kind of interpretation generally aims to explain the child's behaviour in terms of a putative non-conscious wish. Most frequently, the need for defence is explained in terms of the presence of an unconscious wish. For example, the therapist might say that: 'I think you tend to forget your dreams because in these dreams you are able to think about how angry you feel with your father and that you wish to punish him in cruel ways for how he has treated you.'

Reconstructive interpretations aim not only to explain a current state of affairs in the child's mind, but also to give an account of how this may have come about. The reconstruction of early experience in this context is somewhat controversial. While psychodynamically oriented psychotherapists frequently assume that the representation that the child constructs of them is powerfully influenced by the child's prior experiences with caregivers, it does not by any means invariably follow that these experiences find direct expression in such representations. For example, a child might see the therapist as a critic who persistently undermines the child's sense of confidence and well-being. He is thus evidently externalizing an internal representational figure who constantly bombards the self with disparagement and criticism. Such a representation may well be the product of defensive manoeuvres rather than an indication of the presence of a severely critical adult figure in the child's past. Thus, the therapist might safely interpret that 'I think you are worried about my criticizing you because there is a voice inside your head which constantly says that you are such a naughty child that nobody could love you'. It would probably be unwise to assume, however, that such a critical figure was actually part of the child's earlier experience. Such an 'internal object' is more likely to be a split part of the child's self-representation which may indeed be based on the internalization of an actually destructive and aggressive caregiver, or it may be a disowned destructive or aggressive part of the child, separated off precisely because the perceived kindness of the actual parent made such aggressive impulses seem totally unacceptable and intolerable to the child. In either case, what needs to be addressed in reconstructive interpretations is how unacceptable a child finds even a small amount of residual aggression and destructiveness which has remained as part of the self-structure: the unacceptability of such feelings towards the therapist/father and how the child's anxieties about, say, burglars link to his image of father responding to his angry feelings. Through verbalization of these defensive aspects, the child is gradually able to modify his internal standards for acceptable ideas and feelings and take on board the destructive aggression as part of his self-representation, leading to greater integration and flexibility in his psychic functioning.

Thus, the therapists' interventions tend mostly to combine a focus on defences, wishes and past or current experience. What all such interventions have in common is a focus on the child's emotional experience in relation to these domains. The therapeutic action of psychoanalytic psychotherapy is assumed to be 'work in the transference' (Strachey, 1934). The child's interaction with the therapist becomes increasingly invested with affect as the therapy progresses, as internal representations of relationships find expression in the relationship with the therapist. 'Working through', helping the child to understand his reactions to the therapist in terms of anxieties, conflicts and defences, is regarded as the essence of therapeutic work. The development of the transference is facilitated by: (a) the therapist's neutrality; (b) emotional availability (attunement to the child's predicament); (c) encouragement to freely express thoughts and feelings; (d) the regularity and consistency of the therapeutic structure; and (e) the child's underlying perception of the therapist as a benign figure (Chethik, 1989). The transference relationship offers a window on both the nature of the child's relationship with the caregiver, as experienced by the child, and aspects of the child's experience of himself – particularly those aspects which the child experiences as unacceptable and wishes quickly to externalize on to the figure of the therapist. The role in which she finds herself enables the therapist to learn about the child's internal world. Distorted mental representations are identified, clarified and understood and ideally reintegrated with the mature aspects of the child's thinking (Abrams, 1988).

For example, shy, frightened and withdrawn, a boy aged eight, who was referred because of his depression, developed an exceptionally acrimonious relationship with his therapist. The therapist frequently found herself shamed and ridiculed, endlessly failing in the tasks set by the child, accused of being stupid and so on. The child simultaneously bullied and patronized the therapist. The therapist gently showed the child how he often considered himself not to be good enough and placed himself in situations where this would be all too evident. Gradually the idea was presented that being insignificant and 'no-good' was preferable (safer) since it avoided the even more unpleasant possibility of observing that the therapist or his parents might be disappointed with him. Eventually, the problem was traced back to his guilt feelings about his sadistic aggressive feelings towards his younger brother whose birth precipitated his depressive episode.

Termination of the treatment is signalled by (a) symptomatic improvement; (b) improved family and peer relationships; (c) the ability to take advantage of normal developmental opportunities; (d) the ability to deal with new environmental stressors; and (e) the ability to use the therapy more effectively (experience the therapy as helpful, allow the therapist's interpretive work to continue, express feelings more readily, show gratitude as well as criticism and anger, show insight, humour and healthy self-mockery etc.) (Kernberg, 1995). 'Traditional' psychodynamic treatment of this sort is rarely prolonged; much may be achieved in once-weekly meetings over one year, although treatment length is generally eighteen months to two years (Fonagy and Target, 1996c).

Therapeutic approaches addressing disorders of mental processes

Not all childhood disorders respond readily to psychotherapeutic intervention. Diagnostically these children are often categorized as narcissistic, borderline or severely conduct disordered and delinquent. Over recent decades the psychodynamic approach has been extended to these children as well (see for example Bleiberg, 1987, 1994a; 1994b; Marohn,

1991; Rinsley, 1989). While from a psychodynamic perspective most children with so-called neurotic disorders may be understood in terms of distortions of mental representations of either self or other (Sandler and Rosenblatt, 1962), the distorted ideas with which more severely disturbed children tend to present cannot be readily addressed solely by interpretive psychotherapeutic work. Ideas that in less severely disturbed children appear to be repudiated (aggression or aggressive sexual ideation) are often consciously accessible for such children; insight into these seems of little therapeutic relevance. Defences, as normally conceived, are often hard to identify. Referring to the child's anxiety rarely makes the child feel understood, it simply leaves him confused. Psychodynamic understanding of these children is possible if we assume that defensive operations for this group do not simply entail the modification of specific ideas and feelings but rather the mental processes responsible for generating the mental representations (Fonagy *et al.*, 1993). For example, children traumatized by their caregivers find contemplating the caregiver's feelings and ideas intensely painful since, at least in their eyes, these must involve the caregiver's wish to harm them (Fonagy, 1991). They thus defensively inhibit the psychological functions (mental processes) responsible for generating representations of mental states, at least in the context of attachment relationships (Fonagy et al., 1995).

The therapeutic approach required to address problems of inhibited mental processes is qualitatively different from those which may be helpful in treating neurotic children. The therapist's task is to make the child feel once again that it is safe to make full use of his mind. It may be assumed that most mental processes are, at least potentially, available and the free exploration of thoughts and ideas serves to disinhibit the child's pervasive defensive stance. Therapeutic approaches with such children have increasingly emphasized the promotion of opportunities for playing with ideas (Fonagy and Target, 1996b). To some degree the therapeutic approach is unchanged. It is the aim of therapy which is modified (Fonagy and Target, 1998). Neither the recovery of repressed memories or feelings nor arriving at an understanding of unconscious reasons for their avoidance is relevant to therapeutic change. The very process of achieving understanding or the very act of contemplating feelings and ideas may, in and of themselves, assist severely disturbed children in recovering their capacity to regulate, organize and represent mental states. Some techniques required to achieve this end have been previously systematically excluded from psychodynamic work with neurotic children because of their expected interference with therapeutic neutrality.

Effective interventions are surprisingly simple and include strategies such as (a) the enhancement of reflective processes through observation and verbalization of the child's feelings; (b) the enhancement of impulse control through helping the child identify ways of channelling impulses into socially acceptable forms of behaviour; (c) building cognitive self-regulatory strategies through symbolization and metaphor and by the demonstration of the therapist's own capacities for the modulation of experience through reflective thinking and talking; (d) generating interest in the mental states of others often, at least initially, by focusing on the child's perception of the therapist's mental state; (e) developing the child's capacity to play, at first with objects, then with others and finally with feelings and ideas; and (f) the demonstration to the child of multiple ways of seeing physical reality and so on (Bleiberg *et al.*, 1997). Looked at in this way, psychodynamic therapy is no longer considered a predominantly insight-oriented, conflict-solving psychological treatment, but rather a developmentally based mentalization-enhancing approach. It may link diverse therapeutic orientations such as systemic family therapy and cognitive behavioural treatments (CBT). For example, both CBT and mental-process-oriented psychodynamic psychotherapy aim to enhance the child's capacity to organize and structure experiences. The difference lies in the focus of the cognitive approach on particular mental schemata while the psychodynamic approach aims at promoting a broad set of capacities. We expect that an important component of the effectiveness of both therapeutic orientations may be mediated through the rekindling of the child's confidence in the self-organization of internal states. A more focused approach is likely to be more appropriate to children with less pervasive dysfunction. There is as yet no evidence available to substantiate this kind of distinction.

Conclusions

Psychodynamic psychotherapy has a well-developed and helpful body of theory which has inspired many generations of clinicians. Psychodynamic ideas are applied in contexts well beyond the treatment of psychiatric disorders: in psychology, other social sciences, literature, the arts and so on. Psychodynamic psychotherapy is one of the oldest theory-driven forms of psychological treatment of mental disorders (probably antedated only by hypnosis). Nevertheless, in terms of empirical investigations of either its underlying constructs, or its therapeutic outcome, it is still in its infancy.

The shortcomings of psychodynamic approaches include: (a) the absence of operationalization; (b) the uncritical application of the approach to a wide range of disorders ('one size fits all'); (c) limited sound evidence of efficacy; (d) an over-reliance on individual case reports; (e) vagueness of treatment goals; (f) the possibility of unnecessarily prolonged treatments; (g) significant heterogeneity of therapeutic approaches within this category defying integration and rationalization; and (h) an antagonism on the part of many psychodynamic practitioners to the idea of systematic evaluation and scrutiny.

There are many of us, however, who notwithstanding our awareness of the current limitations of the approach remain convinced of its unique value, not just as a methodology for the study of the psychological difficulties of childhood but also as a method of clinical intervention with children whom we find it hard to reach using other methods. Psychodynamic child clinicians are for the most part well aware of the tremendous challenge they face in persuading healthcare organizations, as well as consumers of services, of the unique value of their approach. Considerable work remains to be done but a new culture of research is now emerging within the psychoanalytic community (Emde and Fonagy, 1997). It is, we believe, a realistic hope that over the next decade substantial evidence will emerge which will delineate the specific value of the approach for the long-term development of children with psychological disorders. Work is already under way at a number of centres internationally and time will tell whether psychodynamic treatment works, and if so, for whom.

The current volume is an example of this kind of enterprise. The originators and practitioners of mother- child and father–child psychotherapy are both willing and able to submit their approach to serious and rigorous empirical study. The process of evaluation follows a set of ordered sequential steps (Roth and Fonagy, 1996). It begins with clinical innovation, which involves the development of a new idea in the clinical setting that may be helpful to patients. Mother–child and father–child psychotherapy as such is an inspired innovative approach. The second step involves case reports that document the intervention and its purported benefits in terms of a specific hypothesized outcome. Mother–child and father–child psychotherapy has an ample supply of such reports, a number of which are listed in the bibliography at the end of this volume. The third level involves case series that are normally orchestrated by the originator of the treatment in collaboration with colleagues who he or she has personally trained. Miriam Ben-Aaron has trained a generation of child clinicians in Israel who have learned to use her technique accurately and effectively. In so doing, a time frame for the therapy and expectations about therapeutic change have evolved. The fourth step is prospective pre–post studies that measure the patients prior to and after the intervention to document the nature and extent of the changes. The provision of a formal manual that fully describes the treatment process, such as the current volume, is an essential part of this kind of inquiry. The use of video recording, routine in mother–child and father–child psychotherapy, is a further essential precondition for the evaluation of a treatment approach. The next steps will have to include studies of the effectiveness of the therapy measured as pre–post differences in child and family functioning compared with a treatment-as-usual control group. Here, randomization to the treatment-as-usual and experimental treatment group becomes central to the internal validity of the study (the extent to which causal inferences about the value of the treatment may be drawn from a study).

Psychodynamic therapists have often been (appropriately) accused of shying away from innovation that involved modifications of basic therapeutic technique. This has arguably led to a fragmentation of the field where those recommending substantial changes to a therapeutic approach feel obliged to abandon basic psychoanalytic tenets. Cognitive therapy and family therapy are two of the most obvious examples. Both these treatment approaches originate with psychodynamic clinicians. By contrast, Miriam Ben-Aaron and her co-workers have achieved what has been perceived as difficult or even impossible in the past. They have created a new therapeutic approach but have done this without severing their ties with the psychoanalytic tradition from which they originate. They have advanced the field by making their approach accessible to empirical investigation and thus potentially strengthened the evidence base of the psychodynamic approach. Further, they moved from global constructs that have created ambiguity in traditional psychodynamic studies to specific concepts which will facilitate the data-gathering of the future. They also distinguish themselves by consistently considering alternative accounts in their hypothesis-generation process. The approach of mother–child and father–-child psychotherapy is clearly better able to take on board the social and cultural influences which we now recognize impact so powerfully on the child's unfolding problems. But most important, they have made a major contribution towards ending the splendid isolation of psychoanalysis by actively considering data from other approaches, particularly developmental psychology. Instead of being anxious that the fields adjacent to psychoanalysis might destroy the unique insights offered by clinical work, they have embraced the rapidly evolving 'knowledge chain' of developmental science, which may be the only route to the preservation of the hard-won insights of psychoanalysis.

References

Abrams S (1988) The psychoanalytic process in adults and children. Psychoanalytic Study of the Child 43: 245–261.

Ainsworth MDS, Blehar MC, Waters E, Wall S (1978) Patterns of Attachment: A Psychological Study of the Strange Situation. Hillsdale, NJ: Erlbaum.

Altman N (1992) Relational perspectives on child psychoanalytic psychotherapy. In Skolnick NJ, Warshaw SC (Eds) Relational Perspectives in Psychoanalysis. Hillsdale NJ: Analytic Press pp 175–94.

Altman N (1994) The recognition of relational theory and technique in child treatment. Special Issue: Child analytic work. Psychoanalytic Psychology 11: 383–395.

Alvarez A (1993) Live Company. London: Routledge.

Bion WR (1959) Attacks on linking. International Journal of Psycho-Analysis 40: 308–315.

Bion WR (1962) A theory of thinking. International Journal of Psycho-Analysis 43: 306–310.

Bleiberg E (1987) Stages in the treatment of narcissistic children and adolescents. Bulletin of the Menninger Clinic 51: 296–313.

Bleiberg E (1994a) Borderline disorders in children and adolescents: the concept the diagnosis and the controversies. Bulletin of the Menninger Clinic 58: 169–196.

Bleiberg E (1994b) Neurosis and conduct disorders. In Oldham JM, Riba MB (Eds) American Psychiatric Press Review of Psychiatry. Washington DC: American Psychiatric Press, Vol. 13 pp 493–518.

Bleiberg E, Fonagy P, Target M (1997) Child psychoanalysis: critical overview and a proposed reconsideration. Psychiatric Clinics of North America 6: 1–38.

Bower T R (1989) The Rational Infant: Learning in Infancy. New York: WH Freeman.

Bowlby J (1969) Attachment and Loss, Vol 1: Attachment. London: Hogarth Press and the Institute of Psycho-Analysis.

Bowlby J (1973) Attachment and Loss, Vol 2: Separation: Anxiety and Anger. London: Hogarth Press and Institute of Psycho-Analysis.

Bowlby J (1980) Attachment and Loss, Vol 3: Loss: Sadness and Depression. London: Hogarth Press and Institute of Psycho-Analysis.

Brenner C (1982) The Mind in Conflict. New York: International Universities Press.

Chethik M (1989) Techniques of Child Therapy: Psychodynamic Strategies. New York: Guilford Press.

Clarkin JF, Kernberg OF, Yeomans F (1999) Transference-Focused Psychotherapy for Borderline Personality Disorder Patients. New York: Guilford Press.

Cohen DJ, Towbin KE, Mayes L, Volkmar F (1994) Developmental psychopathology of multiplex developmental disorder. In Friedman SL, Haywood HC (Eds) Developmental Follow-Up: Concepts, Domains and Methods. New York: Academic Press. pp 155–182.

Cummings EM, Davies P T (1994) Maternal depression and child development. Journal of Child Psychology and Psychiatry 35: 73–112.

DeFolch T E (1988) Guilt bearable or unbearable: a problem for the child in analysis. Special Issue: Psychoanalysis of children. International Review of Psycho-Analysis 15: 13–24.

Emde RN, Fonagy P (1997) Editorial: An emerging culture for psychoanalytic research? International Journal of Psycho-Analysis 78: 643–651.

Fairbairn WRD (1952) An Object-Relations Theory of the Personality. New York: Basic Books [1954].
Fonagy P (1991) Thinking about thinking: some clinical and theoretical considerations in the treatment of a borderline patient. International Journal of Psycho-Analysis 72: 1–18.
Fonagy P, Edgcumbe R, Moran GS, Kennedy H, Target M (1993) The roles of mental representations and mental processes in therapeutic action. The Psychoanalytic Study of the Child 48: 9–48.
Fonagy P, Steele M, Steele H, Leigh T, Kennedy R, Mattoon G, Target M (1995) The predictive validity of Mary Main's Adult Attachment Interview: a psychoanalytic and developmental perspective on the transgenerational transmission of attachment and borderline states. In Goldberg S, Muir R, Kerr J (Eds) Attachment Theory: Social Developmental and Clinical Perspectives. Hillsdale NJ: Analytic Press, pp 233–78.
Fonagy P, Target M (1996a) A contemporary psychoanalytical perspective: psychodynamic developmental therapy. In Hibbs E, Jensen P (Eds) Psychosocial Treatments for Child and Adolescent Disorders: Empirically Based Approaches. Washington DC: APA and NIH, pp 619–38.
Fonagy P, Target M (1996b) Playing with reality, I: Theory of mind and the normal development of psychic reality. International Journal of Psycho-Analysis 77: 217–33.
Fonagy P, Target M (1996c) Predictors of outcome in child psychoanalysis: a retrospective study of 763 cases at the Anna Freud Centre. Journal of the American Psychoanalytic Association 44: 27–77.
Fonagy P, Target M (1998) Mentalization and the changing aims of child psychoanalysis. Psychoanalytic Dialogues 8: 87–114.
Freud A (1946) The Psychoanalytic Treatment of Children. London: Imago Publishing.
Freud A (1965) Normality and Pathology in Childhood. Harmondsworth: Penguin Books.
Freud S (1900) The interpretation of dreams. In Strachey J (Ed) The Standard Edition of the Complete Psychological Works of Sigmund Freud. London: Hogarth Press,Vol. 45, pp 1–715.
Freud S (1905) Three essays on the theory of sexuality. In Strachey J (Ed) The Standard Edition of the Complete Psychological Works of Sigmund Freud. London: Hogarth Press, Vol. 7, pp 123–230.
Freud S (1909) Analysis of a phobia in a five-year-old boy. In Strachey J (Ed) The Standard Edition of the Complete Psychological Works of Sigmund Freud. London: Hogarth Press, Vol. 10, pp 1–147).
Freud S (1920) Beyond the pleasure principle. In Strachey J (Ed) The Standard Edition of the Complete Psychological Works of Sigmund Freud. London: Hogarth Press, Vol. 18, pp 1–64).
Freud S (1923) The ego and the id. In Strachey J (Ed) The Standard Edition of the Complete Psychological Works of Sigmund Freud. London: Hogarth Press, Vol. 19, pp 1–59.
Freud S (1926) The question of lay analysis. In Strachey J (Ed) The Standard Edition of the Complete Psychological Works of Sigmund Freud. London: Hogarth Press, Vol. 20, pp 77–172.

Freud S (1930) Civilization and its discontents. In Strachey J (Ed) The Standard Edition of the Complete Psychological Works of Sigmund Freud. London: Hogarth Press, Vol. 21, pp 57–146.

Freud S (1933) New introductory lectures on psychoanalysis. In Strachey J (Ed) The Standard Edition of the Complete Psychological Works of Sigmund Freud. London: Hogarth Press, Vol. 22, pp 1–182.

Glenn J (1978) Child Analysis and Therapy. New York: Aronson.

Goldstein J, Freud A, Solnit AJ (1973) Beyond the Best Interests of the Child. New York: Free Press.

Golinkoff RM, Hardig CB, Carlson V, Sexton ME (1984) The infant's perception of causal events: The distinction between animate and inanimate objects. In Lipsitt LP, Rovee-Collier C (Eds) Advances in Infancy Research. Norwood, NJ: Ablex.

Hartmann H (1939) Ego Psychology and the Problem of Adaptation. New York: International Universities Press [1958].

Hartmann H (1955) Notes on the theory of sublimation. In Essays on Ego Psychology. New York: International University Press [1964], pp 215–40.

Hoffman L (1993) An introduction to child psychoanalysis. Journal of Clinical Psychoanalysis 2: 5–26.

Hug-Helmuth H (1920) Child psychology and education. International Journal of Psycho-Analysis 1: 316–23.

Jacobson E (1964) The Self and the Object World. New York: International Universities Press.

Johnson E (1982) Principles and techniques in drama therapy. International Journal of Arts and Psychotherapy 9: 83–90.

Kernberg OF (1975) Borderline Conditions and Pathological Narcissism. New York: Jason Aronson.

Kernberg OF (1976) Object Relations Theory and Clinical Psychoanalysis. New York: Aronson.

Kernberg OF (1987) An ego psychology–object relations theory approach to the transference. Psychoanalytic Quarterly 51: 197–221.

Kernberg PF (1995) Child psychiatry: individual psychotherapy. In Kaplan HI, Sadock BJ (Eds) Comprehensive Textbook of Psychiatry. 6th edn. Baltimore MD: Williams & Wilkins, pp 2399–412.

King P, Steiner R (1991) The Freud–Klein Controversies. London: Routledge.

Klein M (1932) The Psycho-Analysis of Children. London: Hogarth Press.

Klein M (1946) Notes on some schizoid mechanisms. In Klein M, Heimann P, Isaacs S, Riviere J (Eds) Developments in Psychoanalysis. London: Hogarth Press, pp 292–320.

Klein M (1952) The origins of transference. In The Writings of Melanie Klein. London: Hogarth Press [1975], pp 48–56.

Klein M, Heimann P, Issacs S, Riviere J (Eds) (1946) Developments in Psychoanalysis. London: Hogarth Press.

Klerman GL, Weissman MM, Rounsaville BJ, Chevron ES (1984) Interpersonal Psychotherapy of Depression. New York: Basic Books.

Kohut H (1971) The Analysis of the Self. New York: International Universities Press.

Kohut H (1977) The Restoration of the Self. New York: International Universities Press.

Luborsky L (1984) Principles of Psychoanalytic Psychotherapy: A Manual for Supportive-Expressive (SE) Treatment. New York: Basic Books.

Mahler M (1968) On Human Symbiosis and the Vicissitudes of Individuation. New York: International Universities Press.

Main M, Kaplan N, Cassidy J (1985) Security in infancy childhood and adulthood: a move to the level of representation. In Bretherton I, Waters E (Eds) Growing Points of Attachment Theory and Research Monographs of the Society for Research in Child Development. Chicago: Chicago University Press, Vol. 50, pp 66–104.

Marohn RC (1991) Psychotherapy of adolescents with behavioral disorders. In Slomowitz M (Ed) Adolescent Psychotherapy. Washington DC: American Psychiatric Press, pp 145–161.

Masterson JF (1972) Treatment of the Borderline Adolescent: A Developmental Approach. New York: Wiley Interscience.

O'Shaughnessy E (1988) WR Bion's theory of thinking and new techniques in child analysis. In Spillius EB (Ed) Melanie Klein Today: Developments in Theory and Practice, Vol 2: Mainly Practice London: Routledge, pp 177–90

Pine F (1985) Developmental Theory and Clinical Process. New Haven CT: Yale University Press.

Rinsley DB (1977) An object relations view of borderline personality. In Hartocollis P (Ed) Borderline Personality Disorders: The Concept, the Syndrome, the Patient New York: International Universities Press, pp 47–70.

Rinsley DB (1989) Notes on the developmental pathogenesis of narcissistic personality disorder. Psychiatric Clinics of North America 12: 695–707.

Rose SD (1972) Treating Children in Groups. London: Jossey-Bass.

Rosenfeld H (1971) Contribution to the psychopathology of psychotic states: the importance of projective identification in the ego structure and object relations of the psychotic patient. In Spillius EB (Ed) Melanie Klein Today. London: Routledge [1988], pp 117–37.

Roth A, Fonagy P (1996) What Works for Whom? A Critical Review of Psychotherapy Research. New York: Guilford Press.

Sandler J (1987) From Safety to the Superego: Selected Papers of Joseph Sandler. New York: Guilford Press.

Sandler J, Kennedy H, Tyson R (1980) The Technique of Child Analysis: Discussions with Anna Freud. London: Hogarth Press.

Sandler J, Rosenblatt B (1962) The concept of the representational world. The Psychoanalytic Study of the Child 17: 128–45.

Schaefer CE, Cangelosi DM (Eds) (1993) Play Therapy Techniques. Northway, NJ: Aronson.

Selvini Palazzoli M, Boscolo L, Cecchin G, Prata G (1978) Paradox and Counterparadox. New York: Aronson.

Simon MR (1992) The Symbolism of Style: Art as Therapy. London: Routledge.

Sroufe LA (1990) An organizational perspective on the self. In Cicchetti D, Beeghly M (Eds) The Self in Transition: Infancy to Childhood. Chicago: University of Chicago Press, pp 281–307.

Stern DN (1985) The Interpersonal World of the Infant: A View from Psychoanalysis and Developmental Psychology. New York: Basic Books.

Strachey J (1934) The nature of the therapeutic action of psychoanalysis. International Journal of Psycho-Analysis 50: 275–292.

Sullivan HS (1953) The Interpersonal Theory of Psychiatry. New York: Norton.

Towbin KE, Dykens EM, Pearson GS, Cohen DJ (1993) Conceptualising 'borderline syndrome of childhood' and 'childhood schizophrenia' as a developmental disorder. Journal of the American Academy of Child and Adolescent Psychiatry 32: 775–82.

Tyson P (1992 December) Neurosis in childhood and in psychoanalysis. Paper presented at the Annual Meeting of the American Psychoanalytic Association

Tyson RL, Tyson P (1986) The concept of transference in child psychoanalysis. Journal of the American Academy of Child Psychiatry 25: 30–9.

Warshaw SC (1992) Mutative factors in child psychoanalysis: a comparison of diverse relational perspectives. In Skolnick NJ, Warshaw SC (Eds) Relational Perspectives in Psychoanalysis. Hillsdale NJ: Analytic Press, pp 141–173).

Winnicott DW (1965) The Maturational Process and the Facilitating Environment. London: Hogarth Press.

Winnicott DW (1971) Playing and Reality. London: Tavistock.

CHAPTER 1

An introduction to the approach

Mother–child and father–child psychotherapy (in the general case, we refer to the child as 'he' and the caregiver as 'she') is a dynamic approach to brief treatment of relational disturbances in young (three- to seven-year-old) children.

The mother–child dyad and the father–child dyad meet with the same therapist in weekly alternating meetings so that the child is attending treatment at least once a week. There are also regular meetings between the parent-dyad and the same therapist. Our therapeutic goal is to foster experiential changes in the interpersonal functioning of the dyad, leading to more satisfying functioning relationships.

The developmental thrust in the child creates a disequilibrium in parent–child relations. This can lead to difficult and strained relationships, which can be very distressing for the parent or the child or for both of them. Contact with the therapist will typically be initiated on the basis of day-to-day experiences of inappropriate behaviour in the child. In spite of these manifest disturbances we see the child's difficulties as mostly reactive, reflecting pathology in the relationship and connected with parental conflicts and/or difficulties in meeting the child's changing developmental needs. It follows that the therapeutic process requires the participation of the parents in resolving the child's behavioural difficulties.

The *therapist* provides a framework of security and, through validation of the existing parental roles and enhancement of the inhibited capacities of the parents, makes it easier for the parents to gain experiential understanding of their relations with the child and to differentiate between their own needs and wishes and the child's needs and wishes. The therapist's support and facilitation, and the active participation of the child in the therapeutic meetings, can help the parent to integrate the immediate affective experiences with the explicit and implicit meanings of the enacted or narrated, conscious and non-conscious, themes in their relations.

As therapists we observe and emphatically participate in recurrent patterns and characteristic sequences of interactions of each dyad, their remembered and fantasized relations, and in feeling states regulating the subjective meaning of the experiences. In the space of the therapeutic sessions the dyads can communicate and co-construct meanings on different levels in their respective roles: from immediate experience, such as enactment and play within the sessions, self-and-other observations, to reports and discussions of what has happened outside the sessions. In the role of 'participant observer' the therapist acts as an interpreter of the dyadic relationships, prompting more reflective and emphatic understanding in the parent and in the child. To perform this function the therapist establishes a safe and secure environment for both child and parent. The key to creating such an environment is to support the parent's role, allowing the parent to trust the collaborative engagement of parent and therapist in the interests of the child.

The therapist, as a participant observer in the three dyads (mother–child, father–child and mother–father dyads) provides continuity to the therapeutic process and helps in the integration of the self-and-other representations of the participants. Aware of her influence, as a participant, on the field that she is observing, the therapist learns about the wished-for and current relations between the partners of each dyad, from the roles in which they engage her and from her 'actualized role responsiveness', an important element in her 'useful countertransference' (Sandler, 1976, p. 45).

The dyad, when helped to be aware of shared direct experiences in a safe situation while supported by a secure relationship, is able to co-construct new, different, behavioural patterns and additional meanings to emotionally significant experiences, along with the tendency to re-create their painful aspects.

The *parent* plays different roles on different levels in the construction of the subjective experiences of the developing child. The parent acts through appropriate responsiveness, emotional availability, affective monitoring and mental presence to share states with the child and help him to regulate these states. The intersubjective relatedness allows, through mutual recognition, the understanding of experiences of self, of other and of self with other as well as reflection on and consensual validation of mutually created meanings.

Parents shape the child's behaviour, and create meanings for the child and intimations of the child's identity, according to their conscious and unconscious expectations, so that the links between a parent's past and his/her present feelings towards the child, the 'ghosts in the nursery' (Fraiberg *et al.*, 1975) can distort a parent's ability to attune to the child.

Through sharing of affective states, integration of experiences and more coherent expectations from relationships can be achieved (Basch, 1992; Bowlby, 1979, 1980; Bretherton, 1987; Emde, 1988a, 1988b, 1994; Fonagy and Moran, 1991; Fonagy *et al.*, 1993a; Horowitz, 1988; Sandler, 1990, 1994; Sandler and Sandler, 1978; Stern, 1985, 1994).

Even in severely troubled families, along with vulnerability factors in the dyadic relations there are also compensatory protective factors, and both may exert either an enduring or a transient influence on the development of the child (Cicchetti and Aber, 1986). There is always some 'intuitive parenting behaviour' (Papousek and Papousek, 1979), and when the inhibitions are removed parents are able to relate to, and take some responsibility for, the different aspects of the child's needs and well-being. The child also shows a readiness to shape his behaviour and self-perception to maintain the closeness with the parent. Both factors stem from the conscious and non-conscious relatedness between parent and child in their previous and current experiences.

For some parents their 'child within' (Sandler and Sandler, 1992) can quite easily use the help of a responsive other, the therapist or the child. Very often the child presents the parent with an opportunity to confront unresolved feelings and conflicting representations by playing them out in the 'containing' (Bion, 1962) atmosphere of the therapeutic situation. A mutual process of giving and receiving empathic attentiveness to other emotionally laden states often develops between the partners of the dyads.

The *child* needs the specific relationship with and participation of both parents. The different functional aspects of the interaction with the mother and father, and the different things which these interactions represent, activate different wishes and fulfil different developmental needs in the child. Motivated by the parent's presence and encouraged by the therapist, the child becomes an active and creative participant who provides the relevant themes to the therapeutic process.

Example:

Nina, six years old and second of three girls, was referred by her mother because of 'extreme changes of mood, provocation and difficulty in separating'. 'She depletes me and leaves me empty', the mother complained. The mother herself is the youngest of three girls. The oldest sister was killed in an accident when the mother was thirteen years old. The other sister suffered from epilepsy. Mother was expected to play a special role towards her father and described him as a 'despotic father who mistreated and insulted others'. The father of Nina is not involved in family life. In the sessions, the mother and child are abusing and hostile and, at the same time, very aware of each other. Mother feels that she is 'manipulated' and coerced by the child. Nina sees herself as 'very bad' and behaves accordingly.

Mother and child dyad – 6th session
Nina plays with animal toys. In different situations and interactions there is a donkey – a 'raging donkey', who is criticizing, shouting at the others. Mother observes the play but does not participate. The therapist labels the feelings of the abuser and the abused. Nina is very absorbed in the drama. Suddenly mother states 'I am like this donkey'. Nina stops playing, is very quiet, then cuddles up to Mother and says 'you are my Mommy'.

The here-and-now emotional immediacy of a very poignant situation for the mother and child allowed them to express affects and brought them into an interaction which was new for them. The therapist conveyed to mother and child that their feelings could be shared and understood. The situation – observing the child's play and the therapist's verbalization – helped mother to experience and (in imagination) to participate simultaneously in different interactions and in different relationship roles in time and place. It was probably the representation of herself as an abused child, and the representation of the 'raging' father in many painful situations, that helped mother to be empathic with her own child and to confront the meaning of her own parental role.

We see two parallel therapeutic processes for each participant in the dyad: one with the therapist and one with each other; both of them are necessary in helping the dyads to engage in the best possible way for them.

The child learns to differentiate between the parents of the past and the parents in the present and to value the parents' efforts, their adjustments as well as their failures, as long as the parents relate to the child and affirm their shared situation. The children value the parents' efforts to be 'good enough' (Winnicott, 1971). Attuned to the parents' needs and wishes, the child plays out the conflictual themes in play, narratives and enactments. Turning them into communication tied to immediate experiences in the dyad and between the members of the dyad and therapist enables construction of new meanings for old role-relations and helps to disentangle the child from performing a role that may not fit his needs. The resulting quite dramatic changes in the dyadic intersubjective relatedness reorganize the meaning and the sense of the different role relationships (Horowitz, 1988), and provide the necessary new, positive developmental experiences for the growing child.

CHAPTER 2

The theoretical framework of the therapeutic model and an outline of links to other approaches

Child-observational psychoanalytic writers, and interpersonal and developmental researchers – H. Sullivan, A. Freud, M. Klein, D. Winnicott, M. Mahler, R. Spitz, J. Bowlby, J. Sandler, R. Emde, D. Stern and P. Fonagy, to mention only a few – all agree that developmental adjustment and maladjustment should be studied in the context of parent–child interactions, motivated by feeling states, from which mental representations of the self and other are constructed.

In Sullivan's conceptualization (1953), of particular importance to us is his view of the interpersonal field as organized through particular experiences formed into patterns of interactions and relations with external objects and with 'personifications' of others derived from previous gratifying and difficult interactions. The relations and their meanings are motivated by needs for satisfaction, contact, exercise of capacities and security, based on avoidance of anxiety. The child shapes and distorts his own experiences, behaviour and self-perception to maintain the best possible relatedness with significant others.

The 'good-enough' mother (Winnicott, 1965, 1971), who makes an active adaptation to the infant's needs that lessens in response to the infant's growing ability to tolerate frustration, plays two important roles for her baby. First, she provides a 'holding environment' within which the infant is 'contained' (Bion, 1962). By responding appropriately to the infant's desires, and by functioning as a reflecting mirror of his experience, the mother provides the baby with a feeling of omnipotence. Second, by remaining in the background during periods when the baby does not need her, she supports the development of a capacity for aloneness and autonomy.

The extent to which the mother is attuned during both these processes is central to the child's development of a coherent mental representation of the self. Between the state of 'subjective objects' (the illusory omnipotence) and the state of awareness of the independent existence of others, Winnicott poses a third state of transitional phenomena and transitional objects, a neither 'me' nor 'not me' space between mother and infant, between fantasy and reality. It is in this potential space – where communication, playing and 'mutuality of experience' comes – about that 'the child or adult is able to be creative' (Winnicott, 1971). It is here that the child and the adult, the patient and the therapist are interpreters of their experiences. The 'infant is in a sense the active experiencer and observer of his own complex behaviour and has to make sense of it' (Sandler, 1994, p. 30).

According to Bowlby (1979, 1980), the child builds working models of his mother and his father and of their ways of communicating and behaving towards him together with the complementary models of himself in interaction with each one. The model of himself that the child builds reflects the representations, communicated in many ways, that his parents have of him. These patterns of a parent and self in interaction become generalized, operate at non-conscious level, organize the subjective experience of current relations and guide the expectations from and responses to others, in an encounter. Role-relationship models are enduring schemas of working models, a 'sort of script of what each may do to the other in a sequence of interactions' (Horowitz, 1988, p. 42). The communications between the mother and the child, and the father and the child – their working models – can be best understood when studied in the context of the interactions within which they emerged and continue to develop.

The transgenerational studies of attachment, such as The London Parent–Child Project (Fonagy and Moran, 1991; Fonagy *et al.*, 1993) show that transmission of security to the infant is specific to each parent. The 18-month-old baby has the capacity to encode independently the internal working models of mother and father. The recent studies of Belsky (Belsky and Pensky, 1988), Clarke-Stewart (1978), and Pedersen (1980), confirm the importance of the father's behaviour for the development of the child. This influence is separate from and additional to the mother–child bond, and it also affects, in direct and indirect ways, the quality and quantity of maternal behaviour. According to behavioural genetics and developmental studies, the personal environment is experienced as specific: the effects that parents have on their children are a product of the differences between the relationships, attitudes and behaviour they show toward each child (Dunn and Plomin, 1991). Although raised in the same family, no two children actually grow up in the same psychological environment.

In Emde's formulation (1988a, 1988b, 1990), the basic motivational aspects of the process of development – the activity, self-regulation, social adaptation and affective monitoring that continue throughout life – evolve and are maintained by the participation of an emotionally available parenting figure and his or her empathic sharing in mutual experience.

In Stern's model (1985, 1994) of the developing subjective experience of the infant, the 'schema-of-being-with-another-in-a-certain-way' comprises a network of schemas that represent the different aspects of repeated interpersonal experiences: sensorimotor, perceptual, conceptual, affective, event sequences and protonarrative aspects. Motivated by object relatedness, attunement to the states of the other, needs of safety and self-esteem, the reorganized representations of these interpersonal experiences can be enacted or expressed as memories, fantasies and/or autobiographical narratives. The parents' schema of being with the baby is composed of representations about themselves as mother or father, as wife or husband, of representations about their own mother, father, family, etc. and reorganized by the interpersonal, lived experiences with the specific baby and fantasies about the baby's future.

Parents with good 'reflective function' (Fonagy *et al.*, 1991, Fonagy and Target, 1997) are able to reflect on their own mental states and to comprehend, anticipate, contain and act on the feelings and thoughts of their infants. Over time and with repeated experiences of this responsiveness, the child learns to structure his or her own experience in terms of mental states, such as wishes, intentions, and so on: he or she increasingly represents his/her own actions as motivated by feelings, thoughts, intentions and beliefs. The parents are therefore providing the mental environment for the development of the child's ability to represent himself and others as feeling, intending and thinking. An 'experiencing self' evolves in the context of the infant–parent relationship through intersubjective processes, and subsequently a 'reflective self' is built through interpersonal relations, both dyadic and triadic, prototypically through play (Fonagy and Target, 1996b; Target and Fonagy, 1996).

A child needs to know his parents and be known by them, as experiencing and reflecting 'other' with wishes of his own.

Links to other approaches

There are several approaches to the treatment of dyadic relational disturbances in childhood, but most of them deal with parent–infant relations. Well known to us are: the 'Infant–parent psychotherapy' (Lieberman and Pawl, 1993) based on the Selma Fraiberg programme, and the 'Brief mother–baby psychotherapy' by B. Cramer (1992, Cramer *et al.*, 1990). In this latter therapeutic design the sources of clinical information are the mother's description of problems, and the way she perceives and interprets the difficulties, in comparison with the observed interaction between her and the infant. The assessment of the 'symptomatic interactive sequence' is considered as a valid tool for understanding and intervening in the mother's pathogenic representations of unresolved conflicts enacted in the current interaction with the infant.

In the 'infant–parent psychotherapy' as practised by the San Francisco group, much importance is put on the emotional availability of the therapist for positive changes in the parent's self-esteem. A 'corrective attachment experience' in the therapeutic relationship introduces and supports changes in the parents' representations of themselves as parents, and consequently influences their interactions with the child (Lieberman and Pawl, 1993).

Muir's (1992) approach to mother–infant intervention is based on the infant's creative contribution to self-development and the mother's positive investment in the dyad's relations.

In the 'watching, waiting and wondering' technique (the three Ws) the mother is instructed to be primarily an observer and follower of the infant's initiatives. While interacting with her infant the mother is encouraged to reflect on her past experiences and their impact on the current relations with the child.

In the supporting presence of an attentive therapist, the dyad is helped to discover its own, unique, relational connections.

There are approaches that focus on the behaviour of the infant as leading toward the change in the mother's representations (Brazelton, 1984, 1992), and approaches that aim to change the interactive behaviour between the parent and the infant (McDonough, 1993) as a way toward the exploration and guidance of the mother's overt behaviour and her representations as parent.

A systems-theory approach focusing on the interactive behaviour of the nuclear family members – the mother, father and baby – is practised by the Lausanne group (Fivaz-Depeursinge *et al.*, 1994), where the therapist observes the patterns of interactions between the members of the family: the mother–child dyad plus one (the father), and the father–child dyad plus one (the mother), and herself. Because of the bi-directional nature of interactions, appropriate interventions at any point of entry can have an effect on the particular partners.

Family therapists emphasize the importance of treating the child, usually older children, in the context of the entire family unit (Sholevar *et al.*, 1989), or in small units of the family as in conjoint treatment (Satir, 1967). Some basic assumptions are held in common by almost all the different schools of family therapy: structural (Minuchin and Fishman, 1981), strategic (Haley, 1984; Palazzoli-Selvini *et al.*, 1978), family-of-origin (Bowen, 1978; Framo, 1992), experiential (Satir, 1967; Whitaker and Napier, 1978), behavioural (Patterson, 1980), and psychodynamic (Ackerman, 1966; Wachtel and Wachtel, 1986). The family is regarded as a psychological unit and as a developing system (Hinde, 1979), with shared goals, emotional bonds and changing tasks and rules.

The family has certain properties that exist over and above the characteristics of the individuals who belong to it. There are family realities and 'myths' as well as ways of interaction aimed at maintaining homeostasis, so that the system's identity is preserved. Families are described in terms of subsystems, with roles, boundaries and alliances among subgroups and between individuals, that provide a context affecting the functioning of the individual members; for example, the degree of their enmeshment–disengagement (Minuchin, 1974). The functioning of a family represents a complex web of interrelated relationships. What seems like an individual problem is usually caused by dysfunctional interactions among a number of people, all of whom contribute to the troubled state of affairs. The problem behaviour of the members of the family – the 'games without end' (Hoffman, 1981; Watzlawick *et al.*, 1974) – is seen as serving the family's defensive needs as a whole. The therapist is an active contributor to the changes in behaviour and in the meanings of family transactions; she chooses the units for assessment and intervention, and uses techniques of constructing and reorganizing transactional patterns alongside exploration of the 'vicious circles' and out-of-session homework assignments (J. Reisman and Ribordy, 1993).

Byng-Hall considers the 'rewriting of family scripts' (1995) as the goal of family therapy. In the 'secure base' of the meetings the therapist facilitates 'improvising' new ways of relating for the family, within various contexts.

The new 'scenarios' are co-constructed in the meetings between the members of the family and between the family and the therapist. The therapist focuses the participants' attention on the significant aspects of the themes brought by them, and contributes to the process of co-construction of the new scenarios.

Our therapeutic design was influenced significantly by the 'tripartite' mother–child–therapist model as developed by Margaret Mahler and her collaborators working with psychotic-symbiotic children at the Master's Children Center, New York (Mahler, 1968) (M. Ben Aaron was one of the senior psychotherapists). The revision of the treatment design has been based on clinical findings that showed that the parent, in order to be able to provide emotional support at different phases of the treatment, must develop in step with the child.

The presence of the mother within the therapeutic situation is most important to the initial understanding of the psychotic-symbiotic child's communications. This understanding comes not only through observation but also through information and explanations given by the mother. The mutual exchanges of understanding between the therapist and the mother support her positive feelings and encourage her participation in the help given to the child. The therapist, and the therapeutic institution itself, has to become a 'mothering principle' to the mother.

This design and the therapist's functions of focused labelling, mirroring and affective expressiveness allow for the development of a more specific relationship between the child and the therapist, which brings with it changes in the relationship of the child with the mother. The changes in emotional interactions can be observed directly, and incompatibility between the pace of progress in the child and in the mother can be counteracted over time. We endorse from the tripartite design and the systems intervention approaches an interactive view of the therapeutic process that attends to the individual and systemic meanings of the child's and parent's current relations.

In our approach to the treatment of relational disturbances in childhood we study the interactions and meanings of relations between the parents seeking help and a specific child, as enacted, communicated and experienced during the therapeutic sessions of mother–child, father–child and mother–father dyads. We concentrate on the specific shared meanings of experiences, in the contexts in which they occur. The ongoing implicit and explicit mother–child and father–child relations determine the different meanings expressed in interactive behaviour, and in the narratives of current and past memories and fantasies. Although the dyad is seen as a subsystem of the family influenced by the 'effects of relationships on relationships' (Emde, 1991), we concentrate only on the interconnections among relations that are actualized within or between the dyads and the therapist. We aim to foster experiential changes and reflective awareness of patterns and meanings of specific, observable interchanges within the dyads, leading to experiences for the child which facilitate development.

The reciprocal influences between (1) the parent's readiness to get help in order to help the child, (2) the child's self-righting tendencies and (3) the therapist's attunement to the needed complimentary roles, all promote the creative developmental processes in the participants.

In the developmental therapy perspective (Hurry, 1998) the dyad, the child and the parent can 'find or create' in the therapist an appropriate 'developmental object' (p. 35) that will contribute to their new and currently needed functioning relationships.

Chapter 3

An overview of our treatment approach: The assessment phase

For whom is our therapeutic model appropriate, and for whom is it inappropriate?

Parents, referred by psychologists, paediatricians, teachers, child therapists or self-referred, describe their relations with the specific child as currently unbearable. Most of them feel incompetent, overwhelmed, very distressed and angry, but also genuinely worried about the situation. They see themselves as coerced by the child to behave in ways contrary to how they intend to behave, and describe a dramatic change in the relationship with the child. Patterns of interactions that once kept the parent and child close to each other are now the source of much unhappiness for both or one of the partners. The children are described as making incompatible demands, seemingly impossible to understand and to satisfy. They are seen as quarrelsome, demanding, clinging, provocative, uncontrolled, excessively compliant or fearful. They show extreme liability, and there is great unevenness in the child's developmental levels, some functions being age-appropriate, some perhaps precocious but others severely delayed or distorted. In spite of the manifest difficulties, we regard the child's maladaptive coping and defensive strategies as belonging to the disturbances in relationships, connected and mutually influenced by parental difficulties in understanding and/or providing for the child's uncontained needs.

The relational disturbances can be expressed and caused by any of the most often encountered states within the dyad:

- The developmental changes in the child may create a disequilibrium in parent–child relations calling for a response that cannot easily be met by one or both parents, given their current level of functioning. This is shown by the discrepancy between parental expectations, based on previous patterns of interactions, and the child's current needs, resulting in frequent misunderstandings and inappropriate reactions;

e.g. assertiveness can be seen by the parent as aggression, need for support can be seen as being demanding, etc.

- The parent, the child, or both, may need active help to free or enhance inhibited processes. Inhibitions of the ability to observe and reflect on mental states hamper appropriate evaluation of the relationship, and appropriate expectations, and can be expressed in restricted understanding of self, the other, and the self with the other. Inhibition of reality-orientated mental processes may interfere with learning and with the capacity to estimate changing meanings and intentions. Inhibition of affect regulation can hamper identification of the wishes of others and meaningful sharing of emotional experiences. Sometimes the building up of missing representations, in the relational context, is needed.
- The child as a 'ghost' can represent a split-off, devalued part of the parent's own self-representation, or that of an important person from the past. The subjective drama, belonging to the parent's internal world, is acted out by two new actors – the parent and the child – expressed in the child's symptomatic behaviour. The child sometimes becomes his 'assigned' role, and plays an active part in its maintenance. The parent–child exchange reveals information about the parent's fantasies and conflicts in the relationship with the child, and about the child's response.

Parents most often ask for help only for the child, but almost all are ready to be involved and to participate in the process when this is appropriately broached with them. The mother–child, father–child and mother–father dyadic development approach is practised by our group as:

- a diagnostic tool to help in the identification and understanding of pathology, as well as a tool for the evaluation of the capacities and motivation of the parents to participate in this kind of treatment for their child;
- the treatment of choice among dynamically orientated therapies for relational disturbances between parents and their (developmentally) prelatency children, whose self-organization and self-evaluation processes are still very dependent on the day-to-day experiences within the dyads and the triad.
- preparation, in some cases, for individual therapy for the child or the parent.

In our experience any kind of improvement in the parent–child relationships reinforces the child's self-righting tendencies. We see it as significant enough to justify special efforts by the parents and by us, as long as the goals are realistically determined.

A period of trial treatment/evaluation can help in learning about the usefulness of the dyadic treatment in mobilizing and enhancing the capacities of the parents. In the safe and sufficiently structured setting of therapy, where the therapist sees the parent as a collaborator, the therapist can flexibly try out many approaches: from supportive guidance, modelling and psychoeducation to psychodynamic developmental understanding, and find out together with the parent how he or she can best serve the child's interests.

Clinical procedure: assessment phase

The therapist's goal in the assessment phase is to understand the child's difficulties with each of the parents, and in the relationship with both together, and to assess the parental motivation and capacity to participate in this kind of help for their child. We are interested in any information spontaneously provided by the parents about the child, themselves, their relationships, wishes, etc. We evaluate the parents' approach and their understanding of the problem situation, the differences in the mother's and the father's stances, their emotional involvement and worries about the present, past or future of the child. The therapist explains what can be learned from dyadic meetings about a child's difficulties, and about possible help.

The number of evaluation sessions varies between four and six. Sometimes information from other relevant sources (medical, educational, as well as from psychological tests) is added. Dyadic evaluations are held in alternating meetings with the mother–child and father–child once a week. In the first parent–child session, the parent is asked and helped when necessary to explain to the child the purpose of the meetings, focusing on the child's needs.

In the dyadic sessions, the therapist observes the usual interactional patterns between the partners and the main themes in their play or conversation. Attention is also paid to the ways in which the child and his parents use the therapist's presence. The parents are encouraged to express their impressions and understanding of what happened in the dyadic sessions. The therapist shares with them her impressions about the child's difficulties and recommends appropriate treatment.

Example of dyadic therapy formulation

The preliminary data collection and assessment of Sam, a 5-year-old boy, was carried out over five meetings: one with the parents, one with the mother–child dyad, one with the father–child dyad, a second with the mother–child dyad, and then with the two parents.

Sam was referred by his mother on the insistence of his nursery-school teacher, who viewed him as 'a depressed and withdrawn child, who avoids new learning experiences, reacts very often with temper tantrums and has difficulty in separating from his mother'. The mother had seen some of Sam's difficulties, such as occasional bed-wetting and refusal to separate from her, but was not worried by them. The father – absent from home, except for weekends, for the past four years since Sam's birth, because of his studies – considered himself not to be involved in the life of the family and of the two children, Sam and a 3-year-old daughter.

The material from the dyadic meetings was evaluated from the perspective of the child's representations of himself, as expressed in his interactions with mother and father, as well as in the themes of his fantasy-play.

Sam with mother – first meeting

Sam chooses to play a card game with his mother and ignores her suggestion that they play with a doll's house. Mother proposes playing with a limited number of cards, to make it easier for Sam, but he insists on playing 'with all of them'. In response to mother's suggestion that he take one more card he answers angrily 'I can't hold them'. Mother's attitude is patient and tender, there is even a kind of compliance with the child's demands. Sam looks very much at ease and asks mother if the horses drawn on the cards are boys or girls, but she ignores the question and the pleasant atmosphere changes abruptly. The boy shows some irritation.

In order to lessen Sam's annoyance, his mother changes the rules of the game and suggests that it is a 'game without a winner'. But when Sam decides to play again, mother refuses and asks, with contempt: 'why, do you want to win too?'. Sam laughs and says: 'yes, I want to be even with you', and moves towards the doll's house which mother suggested earlier. Together they play with a family of bears. To Sam's question as to which is the mother and which is the father, again there is no reply. Sam decides that 'the whole family sleeps in one bed'. To this mother reacts and asks 'who sleeps near the little bear?'. Sam replies: 'Mother sleeps with the little bear and father sleeps beside them.'

He then continues: 'a monster enters the house in he middle of the night and fights with the mother-bear. The monster wanted to kill her! In fact, two monsters came to kill the family – the little girl is also a monster.' Sam throws the girl-monster out and declares 'I threw her out!!'. Excited, Sam continues: 'mother-bear steps on the TV and crushes it because the monster gouged her eyes out, but the doctor put them back again with a Band-Aid'. Mother tries to divert him but Sam ignores her and goes on playing. 'Father-bear does not leave his pillow, he takes it with him everywhere.' Sam and mother, now united, are laughing at father-bear with contempt. After a while Sam says 'the little bear slid down the slide, fell and broke his head, his legs were broken too, with a lot of blood'.

It is obvious that Sam is well aware of the therapist's presence and her attention to what is happening in the room, although he avoids eye-contact and even hides from her.

In analysing the meeting, our impression was that the theme of dominance and compliance is very important in the relations between mother and Sam. Sam knows that as long as he co-operates with mother's wishes, she is available and responsive to him, even ready to change the situation to lessen his frustrations. But mother does not 'see' him correctly enough ('the monster gouged her eyes out'). She is not a 'mirror' to him but a TV set, and does not 'hear' him whenever he needs her to answer his questions ('are the horses boys or girls?'; 'who is the father and who is the mother?'). Mother does not support Sam's assertiveness. She frustrates his initiatives and leaves him alone when he is angry. From Sam's play we can infer that in his view mother denies father his role in the family ('the whole family sleeps in one bed'; 'Mother sleeps near the little bear'). Boys are looked at with contempt ('do you want to win too?'). The little boy has to comply, otherwise he will be punished in the struggle against a strong, winning mother ('The little bear slid down and fell and broke his head') although there is some space for his anger in fantasy-play.

The relationship does not provide sufficient sense of togetherness for the child to develop a firm sense of self-differentiation and gender-identity. His compliance with mother's expectations and needs seems connected with his extreme dependency on her. Although mother cares about him, she needs help to attune to the actual child, with his present needs and intentions, and to let him separate from their ambivalent closeness.

Sam with father

Sam and father are assembling a puzzle. Each one works separately, and in total silence. Sam's task is to bring the pieces and assemble the inner parts of the puzzle; the father's is to build the frame. Sam shows what he has already done, the father is not interested and continues with his own task. After a while, Sam again seeks interaction with father and asks what he should do. Father suggests that each one continue with his separate task. Sam moves to play alone with the doll's house, the same one he had played with in the previous session with mother. Father notices, but does not join in. Sam puts the little bear on the back of a horse (horses were 'boys' in the card game), is annoyed that the horse cannot stand properly, complains that 'the little bear can't sit' but does not ask for father's help. He puts the little bear between mother and father bears and says 'they are strolling together'. Sam continues his play; all the bears are riding the horses; he makes father-bear ride very fast but the bear falls down and Sam declares 'he cannot sit because of the horse's long hair'. Father, who watches from a distance, gives only partial and impractical solutions. Sam continues to narrate his story: there is a cruel war 'between bears and horses, mother-bear is strong and winning ... now she will beat him ... this is father [a horse]'. Mother-bear attacks the horse, 'they are dead, the bears are not dead'.

After a while Sam plays the card game with his father who takes, without asking, the first turn. Sam is quite annoyed but continues to compete. In a 'clever' move he takes an important card from father's hand and with a triumphant smile says 'now we've got you, go on'. Father ignores Sam's joyous pride, wins the game but suggests that 'it can be considered a draw'. Sam disagrees and states that father won the game. He turns to the therapist and tells her that at home he likes to play with Barbie dolls.

In the relationship with the father, Sam seeks interaction but father is not open enough to affective sharing. The boy misses a sense of togetherness with father, who seems unable to alleviate Sam's feelings of helplessness and anger. Sam regards father as inadequate (he 'falls down' instead of 'riding faster' as Sam wishes him to). For the child, the powerful position of mother makes father weak and ineffectual, unable as 'second object' to alleviate Sam's doubts about his identity: is he a horse or a bear? Can a horse-boy be strong? Is he a child of mother and father (the little bear between mother and father when 'they are strolling together')? In Sam's view the relation between the parents is a struggle in which only the strong mother survives (the horses are dead, the bears are not dead'; 'she will hit him').

The therapist's presence helps the child play out his helplessness over the impossible dilemma – he cannot identify with father, who is weak and absent, and reduces the identification with mother because of the danger of losing her, and himself. His frequent temper tantrums reveal his frustration about the present state.

Sam with mother – second meeting

In this meeting, the mother–child dyad spend most of the time in mutual play with Barbie dolls. They both seem very happy with this 'girlish' play.

After a while, in a sudden change of mood, Sam plays with the horses (as in the session with father), and tells mother that father-bear could not ride the horse. Sam tries to put Barbie dolls on the horses but cannot succeed and becomes more and more angry. Mother stays calm and denies his anger, even laughs at him by repeatedly saying 'never mind'. Sam is furious, attacks mother, but tries to suppress his anger. He cries helplessly 'I feel horrible'. He cannot put the doll on a horse and hits the doll forcefully. Mother, still calm, denies his feelings – 'but you do know how to do it'. She withdraws further and Sam addresses her angrily: 'play with me, there must be bad ones and good ones'.

> He asks mother to choose 'the bad ones and the winners'. When mother refuses to choose and to decide who is good, the child shouts 'I cannot stand it any more', hits his own head and says 'this is worse, the little bear is the worst'.

In the session Sam presents his story explicitly to the therapist; the child shows how mother refuses to share in his feelings and conflicts, and how she denies his real need for better integration and for differentiation between the 'bad ones and good ones' 'the winners and losers', and the 'boys and girls'.

In the meetings with each parent the child plays out, quite dramatically, his 'basic questions' and shows clearly how much he needs their participation, and not only their presence, to be able to find some answers. We see Sam's difficulties as connected with his extreme dependency on his mother, who maladaptively sustains his doubts about his self-identity and self-esteem. He gets very little help from father as a 'second' object.

The parents need help in order to help the child to integrate positively valued experiences of himself and support his capacity to handle frustration. The child needs their support to find out about his role in the family relationships, and to clarify, with their and the therapist's help, his self-representations, his feelings and his fragile self-esteem.

In the concluding meeting, the parents, surprised and impressed by the themes of Sam's play, mentioned for the first time their concern about Sam's wish to be and to dress like a girl. They had found the dyadic meetings to make sense to them, and readily accepted the recommendation of dyadic therapy.

Some parents are less well motivated to confront their role in the establishment of the child's problems, and to take an active part in helping their child. Sometimes more sessions with the parents, either as a couple or individually, are needed before it is possible to continue with parent–child sessions. Sometimes an alternative therapeutic approach must be considered.

Based on extensive experiences with the assessment/exploration period, we now exclude from dyadic treatment parents with seriously deficient, or missing, ego functions that block their ability empathically to share and reflect on their own mental states, and those of their child, in mutual interchanges. We also exclude parents who find it extremely difficult to accept the separateness of the child and to see the actual child for himself, as well as those unprepared to make the effort to increase their investment in the child.

The first aim of the dyadic treatment is to mobilize the existing possibilities in the family, and maximize the opportunities for experiences that are growth-promoting for the child. Any changes, even small ones, in this direction are significant for the parent–child relations and therefore for the child's developmental needs, and justify a trial learning period with most of the families.

CHAPTER 4

Establishing the frame of the treatment, and the formation of therapeutic alliance

Relational and interpersonal disturbances in the parent–child dyads are the focus of the treatment. In our design the dyads of the mother–child, father–child and mother–father meet alternately with the same therapist in the same physical setting. Each dyad is seen not less than once every two weeks, so that the child attends the meetings at least every week. The mother–father dyad is seen at least every three weeks. The length of the treatment depends on the child's age, (shorter for younger children), and on parental motivation. On average, there are 20 sessions with the mother–child dyad, 20 sessions with the father–child dyad, and 10 meetings with the father–mother dyad. Our aim is to provide the parent and the child with a safe, non-judgemental, but sufficiently structured context to enable them to participate with more trust in mutual experiences and to explore new ways of sharing.

The working therapeutic alliance is based on an attitude of positive regard and respect, as well as a realistic approach to the parents' current capacities, and their readiness to enhance them at a viable pace. (Our understanding of the working alliance is based on the definition of the notion by Greenson [Greenson, 1967]. The patient is motivated to form and maintain a rational and co-operative relationship, and has the ability to follow the insights of the analyst; is able to communicate in a variety of ways and to observe himself. The alliance depends on his capacity to maintain contact with reality and his willingness to regress into a fantasy world [p. 208].) The parent has to recognize that he needs help in order to help his child, and has to be ready to explore often painful feelings and memories from his own childhood. The therapeutic setting facilitates empathic sharing between the participants, experiential learning, attunement to different feeling states, varied ways of expression, and appreciation of varying, subjective points of view. The therapist helps the mother, the father and the child to express themselves more freely, and to see how the defensive protection from pain and past disappointments has taken precedence over their current potential to find different solutions to conflictual wishes. For some parents, observation and participation in the child's activities in the treatment meetings can be experienced as threatening, and can evoke ambivalent attitudes and negative feelings such as envy, competitiveness or even hostility.

The therapist, aware of the influence of resistance on the conscious and non-conscious wish to 'repair' the relationships, has to act as the guardian of the rightful roles in the parent–child dyad. Through her attitude and clarifications, the therapist explicitly conveys to the parent that his or her role as an adult, and parent to the child, is respected and supported. The parent is invited, as a co-worker, to observe and to try to understand his or her own motivations, expectations and needs, as well as those of the child as expressed in interactions, memories and fantasy. The parent must feel that the therapist accepts his or her unique ways of being with the child and his or her intention to facilitate change.

Positive aspects of the therapeutic relationship become gradually incorporated into the parent's representation of himself as a parent, and are expressed in increased tolerance of different feelings and painful memories. Feeling understood by the therapist, the parent is able to explore some of the wishes of his 'child within'(we view the therapeutic dyadic design as facilitating the development of what Sandler and Sandler [1992] call 'structures of insight' (p. 46). The identification of the parent with the therapist's stance, and the child's presence, enables a 'developmental perspective which allows him to perceive and to tolerate the previously unaccepted "child within"' [p. 47]) and their impact on his perception of the real child. Inhibited resources can be released and some interference with mental processes removed when the present meaning of parental roles is validated and the parent respected as an individual.

For most parents the therapist, as a 'new' and transference object, is experienced as fostering and reinforcing their parental role toward the child, helping them to be involved 'playfully' in conflictual themes, as they become enacted in the meetings. (As defined by Moran [1987], playfulness in normal development is a 'pleasure-orientated flexibility' of parents in interaction with their children, which enhances the child's feelings of competence and increases his 'options for mediating or solving conflict' [p. 17].) In the course of the treatment the therapist has to work within a balanced stance between the parent's unrealistic self-enhancing feelings and the self-strengthening feelings that the participation in the collaborative effort can give. (Idealizing and twinship transferences [Kohut, 1977, 1984], defined as a trusting dependence on the wisdom and power of others and 'being like' the other.)

Feeling supported by the therapist, the child learns very quickly that the parent is willing to make an effort to help him. Almost from the beginning the child negotiates actively and creatively, in play with each parent, the different meanings of their representations and expectations. The child's positive self-evaluation and motivation to communicate in different ways is greatly improved by the parents' participation.

Parental feelings of competence require a reality-orientated observational and reflective stance toward the child's needs in the present and in the future, as well as realistic appraisal of their own needs and potentials. The children not only appreciate their parents' good intentions but are more than ready to participate in mutual 'repairs' of their images of themselves and of each other.

CHAPTER 5

The therapeutic process: the functions of the therapist

The therapist is a participant observer of the interacting dyads *in vivo*, and meets the dyads in the most natural state of being together that can be achieved in a therapeutic setting.

To serve the child's developmental needs the therapist has to support explicitly the parents' roles in relation to their child. She facilitates, and provides a bridge for communication between the partners of the dyads; she verbalizes and translates the meanings of their interactions and relations in the here-and-now; and, through empathic attunement, helps to focus their dialogues on their separate and subjective points of view as they emerge in their dialogues.

As a participant observer she learns each dyad's special 'language' and tries to understand experientially the specific themes of their relations and difficulties. Inhibited mental processes can be released; anxiety and interference with the observation of self and other lessen when the meaning of the parental role is made explicit and validated and the parent is respected as an adult. A kind of 'developmental help' is sometimes provided to the parent–child dyad, through modelling, labelling and facilitation of affect regulation. (Developmental help is practised at the Anna Freud Centre in the treatment of children and adults suffering from developmental disturbances and inhibition of mental processes [Fonagy *et al*., 1993b; Fonagy and Target, 1996b; Hurry, 1998; Kennedy and Moran, 1991].)

The beginning phase

One of the main goals of this phase is the consolidation of the therapeutic alliance, based on acceptance of the parents as collaborators in the treatment efforts, as well as on a realistic approach to the parents' current capacities (see also parent–child dyads and parents' dyad sections). The empathic and tolerant stance of the therapist, and the 'as if' playful atmosphere, enable the parent and the child to feel safe in the meetings. The therapist promotes the parent's positive attitudes, based on his or her feelings of being accepted and understood and, by reducing anxiety and resistance, she facilitates the unfolding of significant interactions in the meetings between the parents and their child and in the parents' meetings.

The therapist focuses the parent's attention on the observation of characteristic patterns of behaviour and on recurring themes in the dyadic interaction; she helps in the process of identifying and attending to their possible meanings, from both the parents' and the child's points of view. The child often needs help to learn about his parents' states of mind in order to be able to understand more accurately their intentions, motivations and expectations. It makes an emotionally very important difference to the child if the parent expresses clearly that he prefers not to take part in an interaction because of its nature and not because he does not care to engage with the child.

The parents are exposed to a kind of psychoeducation that facilitates flexibility and empathic understanding of needs. The therapist has to be respectful of the parent's familiar roles for the child, and of the specific issues unique for the dyad when activating the parent's efforts to modify them significantly for the child's sake. The parent, through identification with the therapist, learns that she can be a watchful observer and a sensitive, interested interpreter of the meanings of ongoing interactions with her 'real' child, in the immediate situation. The therapist helps in translating recurrent familiar patterns by engaging the parent in connecting them with more reflective self-and-other observations, in day-to-day shared experiences.

The middle phase

The parent, 'safer' and more satisfied in her parental role, expresses more freely the 'natural' positive and negative feelings toward the child, together with positive and negative transference feelings toward the therapist and their working alliance. Reassured in the helping role, by feelings of identification with, and secure dependence on the therapist, the parent is more prepared to reflect on her caregiving, growth-promoting obligations towards the child, now also seen more realistically. The parent simultaneously gives and receives help, a position that corresponds to the balance between her (positive and negative) transference and her realistic feelings towards the therapist. The real child's participation provides the parent's 'child within' with possibilities of expression and response. This allows the emergence of wishes experienced through identification with the enacting child, in the accepting atmosphere of the dyadic meetings.

The therapist has to find the right balance between intervention on the one hand (modelling and illustrating behaviour and/or lending observational and thinking capacities – functioning as an 'auxiliary ego' [Sandler *et al.*, 1980] for the child or the parent) and, on the other, being a latent presence for parent and child that can be recruited for the strengthening, sustaining and validation of needs, wishes and roles (self-object, defined as a supplement to/an extension to the self [Basch, 1992; Kohut, 1984]).

In the space of the dyad's relations, the therapist is invited by the parent and the child to play, flexibly, a diversity of roles: the role of an 'expert'; of 'benevolent or demanding authority'; of an 'object' from the past (transference object), or a new useful object: of a co-narrator of the child's or the parent's story, one that guides and values or one that controls. In the process of searching for 'corrected' meanings to old role relations, the therapist supports the parent and assists the child by interpreting their needs from each other and by helping them to confront their potential for different patterns of mutuality in their relationship. Working through that can change these patterns for the parent, and the child is facilitated by the emphatic stance of the therapist and her active availability and creativity (Emde [1990] – 'corrective empathic experiences' are embedded in the therapist's actions and mobilize development. They are expressed through her availability and creativity which are seen as basic to an adult's empathy in the caregiving role).

The emotional state of the parent and the child, as well as the therapist's personality, will influence the intensity and extent of her involvement in the dynamic exchanges of the dyad. From the relational patterns and the affective climate, the therapist distinguishes her own reactions and interprets what the parent and the child need from her (what Kohut [1977] defines as 'objective countertransference'). Most of the wishes are redirected by the therapist for working through back to the ongoing interactions of the dyad; some are directed to the other parent–child dyad, or to the parents' dyad.

Example:
Almost from the beginning, the dyadic sessions of father, Harry (a 5-year-old boy) and a female therapist seemed to be stressful for the father and, in spite of his positive motivation to help the child and the therapist's cautious support, father's anger and irritation were growing. In one of the early sessions father reacted to the verbalization directed to the two partners of the dyad by shouting angrily 'I am here to see and learn from what you are doing and not to do it myself'. The therapist's frustration and uneasiness were understood as mostly expressing the father's ambivalence about receiving 'help' from a woman. In the work with the mother–father dyad the therapist focused on and supported Harry's mother as the one who discusses with the father and the therapist the boy's difficulties and needed changes in the parents' reactions.

The working through in the context of the mother–father dyad enabled the father to make a better integration between his self-representations as a father to Harry, husband and man, thus contributing meaningfully to the child's progress in collaboration with the therapist, seen as a facilitator of his special role as father to the boy.

The therapist is a watchful guardian of the therapeutic goals of development-enhancing help to the child and the enrichment of the parental roles. In interactions with the therapist, special attention is given to activation of the parent's 'reflective function', and the release of inhibited capacities. (Fonagy et al. [1993a] define the reflective self-functions of the caregiver as: the capacity to contain the infant's overwhelming affects; to anticipate needs; to adapt to his perspective and to manipulate the external world to fit it.) Representations of the child and the parent can be reorganized, past and present representations integrated and revalidated in the context of reactivated capacities.

Example:

Nick, a 5-year-old, first-born boy, was referred for treatment because of continuous preoccupation with fears of death (which mother was unable to deal with), and, at the same time, with extreme self-sufficiency. A younger brother had been born when Nick was 22 months old.

Nick's treatment started with the beginning of mother's third pregnancy. In a period of seven to eight months Nick was absorbed in three succeeding themes.

The first theme in that play was about a 'very powerful king [represented by an inanimate object] all alone, and very sick, but nobody can help him'. The play, as seen by the therapist, was chaotic but conveyed feelings of helplessness and anger. The mother played different roles, but insisted on playing the king's parent; any efforts to reach the king were rejected by the child.

The second theme (in the fourth month of treatment) concerned a family of dogs: a mother-dog was deserting and neglecting her two son-dogs. The prevailing affect of anger was much stronger and Nick insisted that his mother play 'a very angry mother-dog'. The therapist, as a narrator of the feelings and possible intentions of the main protagonists, bridged the dialogue between Nick and mother, who, although very distressed, played her part as required by the child. In her individual meetings with the therapist (father supported the treatment but was unable to participate), mother was perturbed and very hurt by Nick's feelings of being abandoned. She was concerned and felt guilty about his representations of her parenting roles.

With the birth of the third boy, the third theme about 'losing familiar mother' – Nick's memories about mother's leaving him to give birth – was enacted. The inhibited mourning process was worked through in play with the active participation of the empathically responding mother. Identifying with the

> therapist, she narrated to Nick, as a baby, how she remembered what had happened, who had taken care of him and how she had felt. Literally crying like a little lonely baby in terror, now with his mother supporting him and also sharing his emotional experience, Nick was able to integrate his lost mother of the past and the mother of the present. This belated mourning, which Nick helped to bring to life, was very significant for the development of new relations between the mother and child.

Through clarification of the alternative meanings to narratives, the therapist turns the interactions between the partners in the dyad into processes that communicate a hierarchy of meanings at different levels of explicitness. She helps the parents and the child to relate the conscious or preconscious meanings to more reflective ones. She helps to translate, for example, behaviour usually experienced as negative, hostile and competitive, into possible intentions and emotions, like those derived from frustrations, disappointments, feelings of loneliness and/or helplessness.

The ending phase

The newly found intimacy of the dyad, and their satisfaction in mutuality, is strengthened and worked through in different contexts. The parent feels more competent and confident in his or her ability to reflect on and to cope adequately with the real child's different needs without the therapist's confirming and validating presence. The dyads, each at a different pace and in different ways, convey to the therapist the feeling that her help is no longer needed in the context of their new closeness.

The parent feels quite confident that the attitudes of observing, reflecting, communicating, negotiating that he or she has practised in the sessions are available as his or her own capacities. The continuous adjustments, based on new understandings of what the child needs and how the parent can act, help to free their relations from distortions, and protect them from restricting fears. The positive atmosphere of the meetings seems to be adopted and transferred to their domestic environment.

The therapist helps the parents to assess realistically and with a sense of security their capacities and limitations in being able to meet the child's needs. The child's enhanced potential for expression, his confidence and readiness to engage in new relations with new objects, protect him and ensure his progress. The therapist lets the dyad go, trusting that, whatever additional help might in future be needed for the child or the parent, the experiences worked through in the treatment have consolidated the force of the positive developmental thrust.

Chapter 6

The parent–child dyads

The meetings of the mother–child and father–child dyad enable the therapist to observe and empathically participate in the complex patterns of their interactions, and to share in their feeling states and in the subjective meanings of remembered or fantasized relations. The therapist concentrates on two parallel therapeutic processes for each participant in the dyads – one with each other and one with the therapist.

The child, supported by the bridging presence of the therapist in the meetings, brings up in many different ways to each parent questions such as: 'how do you see me?', 'who am I for you?', 'how do you value me', 'on what conditions can I belong?'. The setting, by bringing the dyad together, enables the child and the parent to 'look at' and to talk to each other, instead of talking about each other.

The child, as the collaborating object of non-conscious pressure from one or both parents to contain and act out some aspects of their self- or object representations, has been induced to think and feel in accordance with these projections. He can be cast into the role of a 'saviour', a 'scapegoat' or an 'avenger', for a parent, or a 'go-between' for the parents, with variations and combinations of the roles. To be 'chosen' the child must have possessed some relevant attributes such as birth order, gender, temperament, disability, etc.

Playing out the roles on the 'stage' of the meetings with the mother and the father, the child, with the help of the therapist and the parent, can focus on the themes, compare them and integrate his self-and-other understanding. In this process the child often indicates what kind of a parent he currently needs. The parent's more reflective appreciation of the child's mental states enables him or her to respond and attend to the child's implicit or explicit attempts to 'restore' him or her to the appropriate parental role, as their relationship needs.

By working through the same themes with each parent, the child is helped in the processes of differentiation of his self-and-other representations, integration of the meanings of the separate and specific relations with his mother and father, and also a better comprehension of the expectations of the real parent as different from the expectations of the 'parent of the past'.

The beginning phase

As a participant observer, the therapist learns about the partners of the dyads from their interactive patterns and from sequences of relations, as presented in the session. Many of the patterns will have been formed as emotional procedural interactions (see, for example, Sandler and Sandler [1997]) which were initially adaptive but which now lead to distortions of perception and understanding. To modify the automatic procedural enactments the therapist needs to interrupt them, and to focus on their possible meanings through verbalization and clarification of the behaviour. Special attention is given to the labelling of the parents' and the child's expectations of each other, in their real relationship and in fantasy.

The child quickly learns to express ambivalent feelings and contradictory self-representations connected with conflicting parental expectations and to 'present' them for observation and understanding. The child is supported in this process by the therapist's empathic participation and her functioning, when needed, as the child's auxiliary ego.

Example:
Ted, a 5-year-old boy, the second of three children, was referred because of adjustment problems in the kindergarten. He was described as 'very clever, but behaves like a baby, not interested in doing and learning'. Mother complained that it was impossible to understand him ('he is up in the clouds'), either extremely detached and disinterested or very stubborn. Father described Ted as shy 'like myself', afraid of children but also one that 'does not listen to anybody'. It was observed that mother had a demeaning attitude towards the father as a man and treated him as 'another child'. Father was unable to express anger directly, especially towards his wife. From Ted's enactments and the interactions in the dyadic sessions, it was possible to see that the child was caught between divergent expectations and conflicting demands from each parent. The mother treated him as 'her man' – and was very seductive towards him in this role. On the other hand she was critical and very disappointed in him, and saw him as unable to do anything 'properly'. The father was warm towards the child but acted as an incompetent friend to him. Ted expressed his feelings of confusion and loneliness and his desperate need for a protective and directing environment.

In one of the early meetings with father, Ted plays by himself with a little doll that is driving a car. When the baby driver runs over a little bear, others shout at him, are very angry and want to put him in prison. When the therapist says that 'maybe the baby driver is too small to be on his own without parents to take care of him', Ted responds by putting barriers around the car and the driver. Among the different objects that surround the driver he deliberately places a small toilet. Then he gets up, runs to the toilet and comes back. Father asks Ted to go and flush the toilet. The boy ignores this but takes the baby doll and pushes it against the barriers for some time. When father, who repeats his request several times, turns to the therapist in despair ('you see'), she suggests that 'maybe Ted needs to be told in a determined and clear way?'. Ted reacts with a 'strong barrier is needed ... made of steel'. Father takes him by the hand and Ted runs happily to the toilet and flushes it.

The following week, in a session with mother, Ted plays with exactly the same toys. This time the car was given to him by 'a sister who gave him permission'. He drives only when there are green lights, 'now that he knows'. Mother is pleased and Ted is also pleased with himself that he is doing things 'properly' and according to the rules. He plays that he 'may see many interesting things'. Mother, who values 'clever children who learn' is very satisfied with him.

With the therapist's help in this interaction, the child feels better understood, and, when supported by the father, can face some of the mother's expectations. Both parent and child try to engage the therapist as their partner and to test the limits of her acceptance and recognition. The parent, reassured by the working alliance and feelings of a supportive identification with the therapist, is more ready to confront the underlying motives and feelings in the child's presenting behaviour and to reflect on their meanings.

The maladaptive procedures are often modified directly, sometimes dramatically, without requiring the stage of 'corrective empathic experiences' between the therapist, the parent and the child.

Example:
Andy, a four-year-old boy, was described by his mother 'and everybody that knows him' as impossible. The mother, a young woman, seemed afraid of the boy. The father was always 'busy at work'. The therapist sees in the dyadic meetings a lonely and angry boy with the mother, and a lonely and contact-seeking boy with the father, who had spent most of his childhood in an institution. It is noticed almost from the beginning that the father is ambivalent about the possibility of playing with the child in the sessions. He is very excited about it but seems afraid. The child lures him into this difficult situation while the father hesitates to activate memories that are probably very distressing.

In order to 'enter' the subjective meaning of their communication, the therapist tactfully conveys to the father her understanding of his hesitation about being 'accepted' and 'allowed' to play. She also conveys that he is needed as a playing father – a partner to his son. The father feels understood and is able to identify with the child when supported in his parental role. The experience of togetherness in the accepting atmosphere of the sessions has a very positive influence on the father–son relationship and promotes growth for both of them.

During the treatment there are many opportunities for the father to work through the meanings for him of being a father to a son. It is understood that the father, through identification with his own father, who had abandoned the family, and by 'loyally' doing what his father did to him ('not being there' and 'not playing'), disavows the traumatic separation and any differentiation between the past and the present role relations. The therapeutic situation helps the father to look at and define his own view on parental roles and to 'repair' the past through new experiences.

The middle phase

In the atmosphere of 'playfulness' and safety, the therapist provides boundaries, as well as containment in situations that arouse anxiety and pain. (According to Bion's model [Bion, 1962], the infant projects his uncontrollable emotions [the contained] into mother who, as an effective container, can successfully deal with and transform them. The infant receives them back 'detoxified'.) She is a kind of 'beacon of orientation' (Mahler *et al.*, 1975) to the child and the parent; they both need the therapist's accepting and flexible guidance toward new ways of being, and the limits she sets, to be able to confront painful experiences and to focus on each other's needs. The trusting dependence on the therapist, developed during the therapeutic process, helps the parents to identify with what the child plays out. Pieces of incoherent memories, images and maladaptive defensive solutions can be explored and rearranged in mutually constructed play scenarios and narratives.

Example:
Amy, an 8-year-old girl, a few months into dyadic treatment presented many problems that could be understood as different ways of conveying to the adults taking care of her that she was not being helped properly.

She had already been 'sent' by her mother over many years to different kinds of treatment for undefined problems. For example, she receives special learning help that started before her school years and, in spite of it, and very high intelligence scores, she is an extremely slow learner. Amy was socially accepted by her peers. Adults saw her as a 'deprived child'. The mother evoked similar feelings in the therapist, although she described her childhood with parents and teachers as very happy. Mother seemed attuned to the girl and interested in helping her, but there was no closeness between them. As observed in the meetings, mother 'performs' her duties toward the child as if not capable of intimacy; it seems that a defensive distance must be kept. The subject could not be touched in work with the mother.

Amy brings her homework to one of the dyadic sessions, and asks mother to help her. Mother looks quite disturbed and refuses. Amy turns to the therapist, who explains that it looks to her that Amy wants mother to help. Supported by the therapist, mother and Amy discuss the subject and mother brings up a memory about her teacher that scared her. Following this meeting the mother, in her individual sessions, slowly recalls many episodes with her teacher-mother, who abused her physically and sexually. In the dyadic meetings, mother starts to relate to Amy's stories and play with recollections from her own childhood, co-constructing, with the child, her 'revised' autobiography. Guided by the therapist they find out in this way that giving and accepting help is not 'dangerous'.

The learning process for the parent and the child is mostly experiential, and facilitates the integration of expectations into a more comprehensive understanding. There is a change in the way that problematic situations are thought about and coped with, enabling the child or the parent to do for himself what the therapist had first done for or with him. (The change is made possible through 'transmuting internalisation' [Kohut, 1984].)

There are many verbal and non-verbal regulating and facilitative aspects in the dyadic encounter; the 'as if' quality of the situation, the validating 'role responsiveness' and the immediacy of the therapist's empathic availability all help the parent to assimilate the experiences within the session and to gain a sense of competence. (In Sandler's formulation [Sandler, 1976], there is a complementary function in the role relationship between the patient and the analyst in which the patient casts the analyst in a role in addition to the role in which he casts himself. The analyst's 'role-responsiveness' is a crucial element in his '"useful" countertransference' [p. 45].) The resulting increased frustration tolerance, as well as the attention given to the current relationship, help both parent and child to feel more confident in their mutual dealings and communication. With the therapist's help, rigid patterns and conflicting themes can be reviewed from the parents' and the child's point of view with the aim of initiating changes in their emotional exchanges and the co-construction of new meanings for old role relations.

Some children continue to 'perform' their role for the benefit of the parent, not yet ready explicitly to acknowledge the change.

Example:
Dan, a boy of four and a half years, was referred because of extreme changes of mood, girlish behaviour and temper tantrums. According to the mother, there was a hereditary vulnerability in her family that affected only male members. In the treatment the boy persistently elaborated on themes connected with self-identity and self-representation.

> In one of the dyadic meetings with the father (after almost eight months of work) the child announced joyfully to father and the therapist: 'now I know that I am not a girl, but Mommy is not allowed to know it yet'. To 'protect' the child, the mother unwillingly conveyed to him that he was a girl and induced him into acting and feeling in accordance with the projection. To 'cure' the mother the boy was ready to continue to participate in the rituals until she was helped emotionally to liberate him from the role.

The therapist has to guide the parent to engage the child and to operate within, and only slightly above the frame of the child's capacity to understand and to express himself. (Vygotsky [1978] defined the 'zone of proximal development', where the caregiver serves as a base of information and facilitates the child's efforts to formulate his own interpretation of a situation by correctly evaluating the child's developmental possibilities and guiding him one step forwards.) The parent's growing empathic appreciation of the child's mental states and his developmental capacities enable him or her better to integrate his or her representations of the child. Some parents are ready, early in treatment, creatively to encourage the child to participate actively as a narrator and an interpreter of their mutual experiences.

The parents learn to value emotionally their present relationship and interaction with the child as he is and to approach positively their own and their child's current capacities. The working through takes place in the child's interaction with his mother and father about the pertinent themes. It is elaborated in play and 'discussions' about these themes in different settings and with different partners, thus reinforcing the child's disentanglement from previous maladaptive roles. The parents bring their experiences from the dyadic sessions to the joint or separate meetings with the therapist.

The final phase

The final phase is influenced by the fact that the parent and the child are terminating the treatment simultaneously. The issues of separation and loss mobilized by the ending of the relations with the therapist seem, quite often, more relevant to the parent than to the child – who stays with the parent. The feelings of sadness and mourning are given appropriate space within the context of the parents' feelings of competence and trust in their role. The meanings of the termination for the dyad are discussed – as well as the different roles that were needed from the therapist during the treatment and which are now no longer needed. The most important indication that termination is appropriate is the parents' willingness actively to face and explore their potential and capacities, and to take responsibility for their strengths and weaknesses as parents. They are also more able to approach the child's way of experiencing things from a reflective stance. Feeling less guilty, they also learn that the child responds eagerly to their good intentions.

Supported by the parents, the child feels free to use his current capacities in new growth-promoting relations in his daily life beyond the therapeutic situation. His relations with his peers and other adults help in working through, in the better understanding of the expectations of self and others, and in his improved capacity to regulate and express affect. The parents and the child no longer need the bridging and translating function of the therapist to sustain their feelings of separateness and their unique relatedness.

The dyadic encounter, embedded in the emotional climate of mutual appreciation, influences and shapes the necessary development of the child's self-representation, self-differentiation, and his self-evaluating and self-monitoring capacities. The parents, by relating to the initiatives of their real child, fulfil as best as they can their role in his development of identity and subjectivity.

CHAPTER 7

The work with parents outside the sessions with the child

The aim of the regular separate meetings of the therapist with the mother–father dyad is to help the parents help their child. The meetings enable the parents to express more freely their conflictual feelings and the painful memories triggered by the parent–child sessions, and to reflect on them in the presence of the 'second other' for the child, who is the marital partner for the parent. The meanings of the different role relations between the parent and the child, and the subjective understanding of them, can be looked at in the safe atmosphere of the sessions provided by the therapist. For example, the child can be cast in the role of a 'go-between' prompting the parents to mend their relationship, or can be drawn into their rivalry struggles and loyalty dilemmas.

The parents, guided by the therapist to focus on what is close to their awareness, help each other to reflect on their own and their child's possible understanding of intentions and wishes. The therapist stresses their different ways of expression or defensive avoidance of expression, of negative affects and personal needs. Individual meetings with each parent are sometimes added in order to facilitate the therapeutic process.

Example:
Eric, a slow-to-thrive, passive, 3-year-old boy was seen in mother–child and father–child alternating weekly sessions for three months. His parents were seen together once every two weeks. The therapist noticed that the father was very reserved with the child and made special efforts not to be touched by the boy. Any advances from the child toward close physical contact with the father were angrily 'brushed aside' and rejected.

In the fourth session with the parents, the mother describes her son's growing activity and new curiosity. The therapist takes the opportunity to talk about the child's age-appropriate initiatives and explorations as well as his active contact-seeking. She encourages the parents to reflect upon the possible wishes behind the child's behaviour.

> In the following mother–father meeting, father spontaneously announces that he knows now why he was so angered by the boy's new approaches to him. It reminded him of intrusive, frequent medical examinations that he had undergone in his childhood, because of his ill health. The atmosphere of safety and acceptance in the parents' meetings, and the interaction in the dyadic sessions, activated the father's memories and enabled him to reflect on and make connections between his reactions and the feelings towards his son.

The growing awareness of separateness, and the differing needs of the parents and the child, enable the parents to disentangle the child from his special roles for the parents. The parent often finds, in the process, active support from the marital partner. The genuine wish to understand the meanings of their child's enactments enables the examination, in the meetings, of distorted representations of the 'real' child.

The parents bring to the meetings their special intimate closeness to the child as well as their factual knowledge and fantasies of the past and present; the therapist, as a specialist, orientates their effort in the child's best interests. The positive relations between the parents and the therapist derive primarily from the parents' feelings that in spite of some failures they can be understood and accepted as 'helpers' – important and unique in helping their child.

In contrast with the parent–child meetings, where the child's activities sometimes require the therapist to model interactions by demonstrating behaviour, setting an example or initiating solutions, in the parent-dyad meetings the therapist presents the parents with useful and relevant information and waits for them to work on it at their individual pace, and in the context of their specific experiences with the child. In this kind of psychoeducation the parents are helped to be better observers of their habitual interactions with the child, to focus on their differing meanings and to pay attention to possible connections between past and present relations. The mutual efforts to formulate relevant questions and tentative answers has an important emotional impact on the parent–child relation. Discussions of the child's possible intentions, affective reactions and defensive acting-out enhances the parent's reflective stance towards the child's 'questions' and understanding of parental reactions.

When encouraged, the parents often know best how to inform the child about their expectations and intentions in a creative way, and how to explain for example what the acceptable limits of difficult behaviour are for them. The readiness actively to support the child's greater autonomy must have been based on a realistic appraisal by the parent of his/her potential and needs as well as on feelings of increased competence and commitment. As for the children, their mother and father can be forgiven many times when their good intentions are understood and mutual sharing is experienced.

The initial phase

The main task of this phase is the establishment of a firm working alliance between the parents and the therapist to serve the child's needs. The therapist learns, from this perspective, about each parent's ways and wishes as well as resistance to change. The therapist tries to supply the necessary skills through psychoeducation, and to lessen the inhibitions of existing capacities through interpretations. Most important, the therapist follows the individual pace of each parent and supports the helping interactions between them. The parents test how much they can depend on the therapist and how ready she is to support their role as collaborators. Mutual inquiries about the child's reactions facilitate parental participation and build up trust. Many themes triggered by the child are brought up, the child functioning as a 'window' on to memories and painful as well as happy feelings. Any understanding gained by the parents is integrated, with the therapist's help, into the context of current relations and more realistic representations of the child.

The middle phase

The parents' natural wish to be in a nurturing relationship with their child promotes their positive use of the therapeutic alliance. The therapist is usually accepted as a facilitator of change. Reliance on her support and identification with the 'helping role' widen the parenting repertory. The parents gain a broader, more balanced perspective on their child's symptoms, and can connect them with the family history and thought about the future. The therapist helps the parents to focus on and examine the degree of consistency and clarity of their new messages and behaviour, which the child has to comprehend.

In the dialogues between the therapist, the parents and the child, consideration of different modes of expressions, and of needs, roles, intentions and feelings, is emphasized. The parents are more willing to be observers of themselves and of the child and to maintain communication with each other. Activated by the therapist, they help each other in the exploration of varied ways of relating, and in negotiation of the possible meanings their behaviour will hold for the child. The safe atmosphere of the meetings enables experiential learning and promotes insight into many themes. These are worked through from the perspective of the parental roles currently needed and what is currently developmentally helpful in the relationships of each parent and the child, as well as the realistic acceptance by the parents of the limits of their capacities to be 'good enough' for the specific child. Sometimes the differences in pace force the therapist to hold separate instead of dyadic sessions with each parent for some periods of time.

The ending phase

The termination of treatment is agreed upon by the parents and the therapist after the meaning of termination for each of the participants, including the child, is discussed. The parents' more reliable feelings of competence in relations with the child, and also confidence about their future role in the child's positive developmental experiences, are seen by us as measures of satisfactory change. The useful aspects, for them, of the collaboration with the therapist are transformed, through identification, into the parents' own ways of functioning toward the child. Flexible understanding of expectations and a more realistic assessment of their influence on their relations with the child, and between each other, are adopted. The parents are encouraged to feel that to come back for more help would not be a failure. This is especially important for parents of young children, where brief interventions, at developmentally significant periods, are desirable.

CHAPTER 8

In summary

The mother–child, father–child and mother–father dyadic treatments with the same therapist form an integrated, dynamic developmental approach to relatively short treatment of relational disturbances in prelatency children. The aim of the treatment is to foster experiential changes in interpersonal functioning, leading to changes in the dyadic and triadic relationships, and development-enhancing experiences for the child.

The treatment setting facilitates the observation of reciprocal influences between the participant partners and the diverse forms of their expression. It enables the therapist, as participant observer, empathically to understand the difficulties early in treatment, and to consider ways that will best mobilize the parents' participation in helping the child, and that will revive the child's developmental thrust. The parent is a respected and vital collaborator in the treatment, and has to fulfil a double function of giving and receiving help. She or he must be ready to explore the meanings of their parental role, and their influence on the relationship with the specific child. The parents' potential capacities and motivations are realistically appraised within a supportive attitude towards their efforts.

The child needs the participation of both parents in the therapeutic process for the re-evaluation and integration of the representations of his specific relations with each parent and for the understanding of their current meanings.

The therapist provides a safe and sufficiently structured context that facilitates the re-creation of significant experiences for the dyads, and the co-construction of new behavioural patterns and additional meanings in their present relationships. The encounters of the different dyads with the same therapist facilitate the parents' and the child's experiential learning through empathic sharing, affective validation, negotiation of different points of view, and identification with an observational and reflective stance.

Positive and secure relations in therapy, as well as the parent's feelings of competence gained through psychoeducation, help to release inhibited processes that enhance parental and caregiving functions. The experiential working through in the different dyads and the resulting insight into the varied meanings of their role relations are assimilated and integrated by the parents and used to serve the child's developmental needs.

The child actively and creatively participates in the treatment process. Supported by the parents' involvement and by the therapist's empathic participation, he enacts, plays, imagines and narrates the core relational themes and presents them for mutual experiencing, sharing, self- and other understanding and communication.

Case studies

The presented treatments were tape-recorded

CHAPTER 9

A five-year-old boy in need of parental help

Therapist: I. Hayut

The intake process

The parents referred their five-and-a-half-year-old son, Adam, for assessment. They asked if he should go to a mainstream school the following year or to special classes for gifted children. They thought that he was so bright that he might be bored in school, and wondered if he needed a more enriching education. They described Adam as having problems in the kindergarten, reporting fights with other children and difficulty in restraining himself when angry or feeling in need. They attributed his difficulties to the nursery teacher, who, in the mother's opinion, was 'mean', and who, in the father's opinion 'did not offer sufficient interest and stimulation'.

The parents are both professionals, each with a successful career. Adam was born as the result of an unplanned pregnancy, after less than one year of marriage. The mother described the experience of his birth thus: 'I was in shock. I had no idea how to hold him. I was helped by my mother to feed him, by my sister to put his nappies on, and by the kibbutz care takers [Metaplot] with guidance and support.'

No development difficulties were mentioned, except for physical problems: at one and a half years old, he had a nystagmus operation that caused the mother great anxiety. Aged 2 years he had some respiratory tract problems. At 5 years of age, Adam exchanged his dummy for a baby-bottle, which he still uses for comfort. He also needs parental comfort getting to sleep. The parents are very proud of his intelligence, and encourage him to show it off.

The couple had no more children, because of their marital problems. At the time of referral they were considering divorce. Mother complained about father's outbursts: on the one hand displaying humiliating behaviour towards her, swearing at her, after which he is calm, asking for closeness as if nothing had happened. On the other hand she appreciates his warmth towards her and to Adam. Father complained about the mother's over-anxious behaviour. They had been in couple therapy but had not felt helped.

During the assessment phase of the dyadic sessions, and in the psychological testing, Adam tried hard to show the therapist that he knew everything and that all the tasks were too easy for him. Faced with the slightest difficulty, he reacted strongly either by acting out or by somatic complaints. It was obvious that he had to experience himself as big, strong and very special, trying all the time to do more than he is capable of, cognitively or emotionally. For example: he drew a train carrying building materials – concrete, timber etc. – that expanded over several pages. The therapist thought he was showing her how much 'firming up' he needs. Adam could not trust the limits that the therapist had set for him. He would ask for more questions, wanted to see more pictures, etc. When restricted by the therapist to his developmental level, he fought, expressing his grandiose and omnipotent fantasies. When he failed at any task he almost collapsed. In spite of his very high intelligence, he had difficulties narrating the C.A.T. stories, and was unable to verbalize mental processes.

It seemed from the interaction of the dyads that Adam was struggling with strong emotions, unable to cope with them on his own. Unable to use his parents to help him, he was left vulnerable to narcissistic insults. He drew a huge house, with 25 windows and a smoking chimney – symbolizing his uncontainable anxiety and aggression.

Dyadic therapy was recommended: alternating sessions once a week; one with the father, the other with the mother. The parents were seen every second week, together and/or individually. Father was seen alone more frequently than the mother, who was already in individual therapy with another therapist. Father and Adam's relationship seemed more troubled and stormy in this phase. The separate sessions with the parents were scheduled according to the material that emerged in the dyadic sessions with the child.

The theme of 'self-regulation', and specifically emotional regulation, was a very prominent problem in the relationship between the parents, and between each parent and the child. Father and mother, as well as Adam, were mutually re-creating and maintaining the ambivalent search for the self with other roles and their changing self-representations – a dialectic between strong and weak, needing and independent, the best and the worse, aggression and hate versus love and compassion.

The parents' histories

A continuous process of re-constructing and co-constructing narratives took place during the sessions with the parents. The material for this process came mostly from the themes enacted in the dyadic sessions. Both parents' stories showed that they used detachment as the main mechanism for coping with emotional problems. Their own parents had not been able to help them to regulate or to communicate their emotions. The father had had to fight, mostly with extreme anger, and mother mostly with paralysing anxiety. The problem of affect regulation showed up in the marital relationship and also in their parental functions. Father's difficulty also caused him problems in his relations at work.

Mother's story

Mother is the younger of two daughters born to a couple who survived the Holocaust. The family history was full of tragic separations and losses. Mother described her own mother as 'a victim of life', always anxious and pessimistic, who had been orphaned at the age of two years. She described her father as someone who had 'fought and survived' and had not become a victim; but she had felt unloved by him, since he preferred her sister. Mother had identified with her own mother's suffering and feelings of deprivation.

When she was 10 years old, she had developed school phobia that lasted for two years. Her mother, unable to leave the house while she was at school, was phoning her frequently. As an adolescent, she had rebelled against her father and finally left home abruptly and went to live abroad. Far from home, she had not felt homesick, but felt guilt about her leaving. She developed some compulsive habits, every evening washing two handkerchiefs to prepare them for the next day, but never using them. At the age of 27 she met her husband and soon they were married. Even before their marriage she had been aware of extremes in his behaviour, a warm and caring stance contrasting with aggressive and humiliating outbursts. Mother saw these aspects of the father as the main source of Adam's problems.

Father's story

Father was the youngest in a family of three boys. He did not have a good relationship with his much older brothers. His parents had immigrated to Israel before the Holocaust, but they had lost all their relatives there. His parents are working-class people, always worried about physical needs and current problems, ignoring emotions and traumatic events from their past.

As a child, father had been lonely and neglected: 'My family had no time nor energy for a little boy. Inside, I always felt weak, not belonging to anyone, but outside, I was the toughest guy in the neighbourhood.' Father described his mother as domineering, intrusive and criticizing, but also as compliant and unable to cope with his anger. Even today he says that he is so angry with her that 'If I could let myself do it, I would kill her'.

Father described his own father as warm and loving. He had worked most of the day and the only time they had had together was in the evenings. His father used to calm him and stay with him before he went to sleep, or when he was ill, but had been unable to stand between the boy and the mother during angry outbursts, and was even now unable to do so. During his adolescence father had cut himself off from the family and, after his army service, left home. He had never telephoned them or told them about his life or his achievements. He never asked for anything from them. Father described all this without any emotion except anger. Several years before his marriage, he was in treatment for three years. He felt it had been only a beginning.

Adam's difficulties were not defined by his parents as problems with self-regulation at the time of referral, even though they showed up clearly in the parents' description of Adam and in the assessment process. Both parents were inarticulate about the subject and were insufficiently aware of their own need for help in self-regulation. The normal developmental tasks of dealing with the do's and the don'ts, with sublimation of needs and wishes, and with their symbolization become difficult to achieve for the boy in the absence of parental partnership. The developmental processes Adam was going through frightened his parents and they were inhibited in meeting his normal needs. Dyadic treatment was chosen on the assumption that by emotionally re-experiencing the process of self-regulation between parent and child, Adam and his parents would be helped to cope better with this task. The parents agreed to this offer and co-operated actively in their role of giving help to their child and receiving help at the same time.

Treatment

Father and Adam – one and a half months into treatment

Adam comes in happily, kisses the therapist's hands and runs to the toilet. Father and Adam missed one session the previous week because Adam was ill.

> Father: 'It has been three weeks and he missed it. He asked me when we would see Itiya.'
> Therapist: 'Maybe Adam and father both missed the session.'

Adam reminds the therapist that she has to bring the big basin in which they light the fire. Father sits on a couch, away from Adam and the therapist.

Adam sits on the floor and prepares paper for the fire (this is a game he played with his mother the previous week, but not yet with father). Father says he doesn't agree with Adam making a fire, and they start to argue about it. At first Adam caresses his father and then he strikes him and their contact becomes aggressive.

> Father: 'You're a weakling!'
> Therapist: 'It seems to me that you are both interested in fighting.'
> Father: 'But it is no fun for me, because he is so weak, weak as a girl; but he is cute.'

Adam hits father's chest. Father warns him to be careful and not to hit too hard, but he himself hits Adam. Then he asks Adam to behave nicely. Adam agrees but then suddenly hits father saying: 'I have been lying to you.' Father complains to the therapist that even though they punish Adam frequently, he still is using ugly words.

> Therapist: 'Adam confesses to you that he lied, maybe it is difficult for him to make promises he cannot keep yet.'

Father and Adam start arguing about the punishment father had given Adam at home.

> Adam: 'Please, cancel it. I have been trying so hard. You wanted me to be a good boy and I did it just for you.'

Now they argue again about the fire.

> Therapist: 'Maybe Adam is confused because father does not know that mother agreed to play with the fire last week. Father says "No" and mother says "Yes", so it is difficult for Adam to know how to behave.'

They are not listening to the therapist, and start another fight. It is so aggressive that the therapist has to stand up and come close to them and say: 'Father now has to put a limit on this fight so that you will not hurt each other. The big person has to help the small person to learn how to stop fighting.'

Father hugs Adam and there is a moment of quiet.

> Adam: 'When will we be finished?'
> Therapist: 'It was so difficult for you, what happened here between you and your father. You want to leave already. Maybe father can show you that not everything is spoiled, and you still can do something together.'

Father leaves the couch and suggests a game of chess. Now they are arguing about who will start. Each of them declares that he intends to win. At the beginning, father tries to stick to the rules, and also to avoid confrontation. When Adam plays well he praises him, and when he makes mistakes he hits him on his head and calls him stupid, silly. Adam calls him the same things in return. There is an atmosphere of fierce competition. At last Adam wins the game.

> Father: 'I have no choice but to surrender to you.'

Adam runs to the toilet. Father complains to the therapist that Adam behaves like a bully. When Adam is back in the room, they renew the argument about Adam's punishment. Father suggests that Adam should decide about it. Adam offers to give up his desserts, but not the sweets. Father says this is not enough.

> Adam: 'You and Mom will not speak to me for a week, and then I will not speak to you for a week.'

Father does not agree.

> Therapist: 'Father has to disagree. It is a difficult and unfair punishment. When a child has to make the rules, he might go too far. This is why father has to set rules that are fair and appropriate.'

Mother and Adam – four months into treatment

Adam enters the room and asks the therapist to keep quiet, as she did at the last session. Mother looks very disturbed by this rude behaviour.

> Therapist: 'It seems to me that you want mother just for yourself. Having mother talking to somebody else is too much. A threesome is not easy to handle.'
> Adam: 'Right. You will speak only to me' (addressing mother).

Adam and mother arrange the dinosaurs on a map. It is a game they also played in the previous session.

> Adam: 'It is a stupid game, right Mum? I will swear only at the dinosaurs.'

They arrange the dinosaurs in pairs. Adam takes the biggest dinosaur, who has no partner, and says: 'This one eats only grass. He's got small teeth, then he eats stones and they help him to digest the grass. Since he was a baby he eats only grass.' Then Adam swears.

Adam: 'If I am cursing you or Itiya, it is only a game.' And then immediately he says to mother: 'Shut up!'
Therapist: 'It looks like the curses come out and you cannot stop them. And it is hard for mother to stop you.'
Adam: 'This Itiya is a bitch.'
Mother: 'Oh, my God!'
Adam: 'It was a joke.'

While playing with the dinosaurs he tells a story about animals who eat grass, and animals that eat each other. He takes care to give each animal enough food. Mother starts to interfere a great deal in his play.

Adam: 'Mom, you know, you're nuts. Shut your mouth and get lost. I'll smack you' (in a deep and angry voice). 'Now you are hurt?'
Mother (in a whisper): 'You think I am hurt?'
Therapist: 'You are angry, swearing, and mother does nothing to stop you.'

Adam continues to talk about the dinosaurs running for food. He begins to calm down and he says: 'all the animals eat only grass.'

Therapist: 'Are you telling mother that there is no need to fight today? The animals eat only grass, and not each other. Maybe you're trying to say how unpleasant it is to fight.'

Mother does not respond. Adam starts again the fight between the animals, making eating sounds. He brings all the animals close to mother's face and says: 'I will eat you' and pushes the animal into her face.

Mother: 'Gently.'
Adam: 'I'm hungry, I'm bored!'

Adam lifts the map and everything falls to the floor.

Mother: 'What a mess.'
Adam (to mother): 'Please, make a pool for the animals to jump into the water.'
Therapist: 'Maybe they feel so hot that they have to cool down, like yourself, and you need mother to help you.'

Mother does not respond, then suggests something else.

Adam: 'I don't like being with you.'
Therapist: 'I think that Adam feels bad when he does not succeed in doing what he wants, and mother feels bad and suggests something else, to change the bad into good. But it does not suit Adam. Like the food that Adam gave the animals, each one with the food it likes, mother will find the right thing for Adam.'

In these early sessions father is moving quickly from the role of a father to that of a child, from grown-up to peer, from strong to weak. It seems that Adam goes along with him, taking the complementary position, so that the game can go on. Adam gets a feeling of control and pleasure from the situation but soon gets very anxious when in the role of a leader. Father supports, maybe unwittingly, Adam's tough behaviour and tries to suppress any sign of what he regards as weakness. The therapist brings in 'reality' by helping father to keep his position as an adult, leaving the child's position for Adam. She tries to achieve this in a way that does not narcissistically hurt either of them.

In the mother/child relationship, Adam is invited by her to take the role of the aggressive and humiliating male figure. Instead of being opposed to it, mother encourages it. It seems that she is re-experiencing her relationship with her father and husband. Adam plays the role projected upon him until he gets frightened and looks for a limit-setting adult. By labelling the interaction, the therapist helps in structuring the situation, which calms the child. The labelling also promotes the reflective functioning of the mother, and the child's capacities for symbolization.

Father and Adam – nine months into treatment

Father enters first and Adam hides behind his back – repeating what he was doing in the last sessions. When in the room he immediately goes to the toilet. Father sits on a couch that has a loose back. He says to the therapist: 'It's falling apart again.' The therapist thinks that he is asking her to prevent the falling apart of things. Adam comes back and starts a fire in a small bowl, placed in a bigger basin – according to the rules the therapist had made before.

The therapist mentions that Adam remembers the rules for lighting fire.

Adam tries to light the fire and father interferes and succeeds immediately. Adam gets angry and swears.

> Therapist: 'You seems angry because you wanted father only to instruct you, not to do it instead of you.'
> Adam: 'You are right. Oh, how right you are.'

He tries to light the fire again, but does not succeed, and then says: 'Now I am going to do something really over the top.'

Father does not react. The therapist shows interest and repeats Adam's words.

> Adam: 'Yes. I am going to make an explosion so big that no one heard anything like it before.'
> Therapist: 'You want father to hear that you want to do something over the top, big, and maybe he will be able to tell you if this is forbidden or permitted.'

Father 'wakes up'. He starts to ask questions about what Adam is saying. Adam tells him he would like to light the whole matchbox at once. Father says it is forbidden in the house, but it might be OK when they are outside, on a picnic. Adam quite quickly accepts this.

> Therapist: 'When father says clearly what is okay and what is not, Adam is eager to accept it.'

They both agree to light one match after the other, and then father lights a candle. Adam blows it out and father says: 'But father also wants to play.'

> Therapist: 'Father remembers how much fun it was to play when he was a child, and he would like to do it again, but Adam needs a big father, so that he can be a child himself.'

Now they start a new game. They plan to prepare a thread that leads into a jar with a candle. They are talking about the fire and about things that make Adam angry.

Adam says: 'I am angry when you do not watch over me.' Father strokes his head. They sit calmly on the carpet and father points out to Adam how beautiful the melted wax looks.

> Adam: 'I am going to make a fluid that looks like lava, and I will pour it here and it will blow over this iron and everything will blow up...but I would never do such a thing.'

Father asks why.

> Adam: 'Because I don't want to die.'
> Therapist: 'It is terribly frightening when you do not have someone to watch over you and stop the explosion. Then you feel that everything is falling apart. Fathers are there to help to keep things from falling apart. Sometimes you are trying to help yourself when you are frightened, like when you run to the toilet. But Adam needs father to help him not to blow up.'

Adam goes to the toilet and says to the therapist: 'I know in my heart exactly when to be in control.'

Adam and mother – nine and a half months into treatment

Adam comes in after hiding behind mother. He looks happy. He wants to start the fire and finds out that there are only three candle stubs left. He complains to the therapist about it.

> Therapist: 'You are disappointed that I did not take care to bring you whole candles, as you wanted.'

Adam:' You are right. How many times do I have to tell you that you should bring lots of candles and matches?'

Mother anxiously starts to suggest other activities. The atmosphere is quite tense and Adam looks frustrated. He tries to light the candles but does not succeed. Mother says how difficult it is for him and encourages him to try again. She then tells him how to do it and Adam gets angry, throws himself on the floor and kicks the chair. Mother looks frightened.

Therapist: 'Mother noticed immediately that it is difficult for you, but she does not know exactly how to help you.'

Mother suggests that she and Adam will try again together. Now they succeed and stick the candle to the bottom of the bowl. They have calmed down.

Adam tells mother and the therapist to close their ears because he wants to tell a story that he is ashamed of 'Get ready! Soon you will control the whole universe. Get ready for the big voyage! I give you my great power to do it, and you will have to control it.'

Therapist: 'You were talking loudly so that we can hear you, but you were also ashamed of it. It seems like an important story.'

Adam asks the therapist to write it down. Mother praises the story. Then they look again at the lighted candles through a blue glass, and both enjoy the beauty. Adam wants more candles and gets very angry when he remembers there are no more. He swears at his mother, says that he is bored and runs out of the room. He comes back with a twig, which he calls 'the branch of hope'. He and mother try to light it again and again, unsuccessfully.

Therapist: 'It is hard for mother to see that her child is not succeeding. When it is hard for her to accept it, it is hard also for the child to accept it.'

Mother tries to explain to Adam very softly that it might be better to leave the branch because it is green and cannot burn, but it is too late for Adam. He starts crying and screaming.

Adam: 'I can't do it. I can't do it.'

Then angrily he turns to the therapist: 'You should bring me two packs of candles next time.' Now mother looks very angry but speaks to him softly, and then sits down in the far corner of the room as if giving up.

> Therapist: 'This outburst is exhausting for both mother and Adam but Adam needs a grown-up to maybe hold him and help him feel when it is enough.'

Mother gets up and speaks assertively to Adam and Adam calms down. At the end of the session Adam refuses to put the things away and says to his mother: 'I have been working here very hard today, so you go and sort everything out by yourself.'

> Therapist: 'Yes, it was very difficult. The branch of hope disappointed you and you felt so sorry and small that you burst out. Mother will try to teach you how to manage and control the setting up of limits, and I will try to help her.'

Discussion

The themes that emerged in the dyadic sessions with the father were similar to those that were worked on with the mother, but the atmosphere was different – aggressive collisions with father, and calm with mother.

In the sessions with father, the therapist, as translator, reflected and interpreted what Adam was symbolically expressing, to help father to be more aware of the child's messages and expectations. Adam tried hard to control his strong and ambivalent affects. He was confused about the meanings of father's outbursts of anger, verbal abuse and warm closeness. Adam needed to enact and to ask significant questions about their respective role relations as father and son. After a few months of treatment there was a transition from power struggles and physical collisions to shared interest in symbolic play. Father had a difficult time being a steady, regulating other, but there were some encouraging expressions of an adult and fatherly attitude.

Episodes of aggression were frequent at home. Once Adam told his father, who came to see him before he went to sleep: 'Sometimes I feel that you are like a truck with broken brakes, speeding down the hill towards me.' For several individual sessions with father, this topic was discussed. Father started to observe and to understand how much he is hurting and frightening the boy. It seems that until then father did not recognize or regret his humiliating behaviour toward the child, and did not understand Adam's aggression and hurt feelings.

In the process of the therapeutic meetings father was reminded of his outbursts toward his mother and his own father's inability to stop him. It seemed that he was looking for Adam to be the strong father for him, one that would stop father from being a bully. He was terribly worried that Adam would be a victim 'like a woman' – a fear from his childhood, projected upon Adam. The 'speeding truck' was discussed in the sessions as symbolizing the frightening feelings of being out of control; as being dangerous and in danger, overwhelmed by strong affects – the way both father and Adam sometimes felt.

The most significant development that Adam went through was giving up his grandiose self in order to get in touch with his parents, as subject to real objects outside. From then on, the relations between Adam and his father became more relaxed. Father was more attuned to Adam's needs, as a small child, less encouraging of his aggressive defences, and more able to be a 'self-regulating other' for him. Father also promoted Adam's capacity for reality testing without too much frustration of the boy's narcissistic needs.

In the following sessions father and Adam mostly shared 'manly' interests enjoyed by both. Adam asked father to buy him a snake to frighten those who were threatening him. Themes of power, destruction but also protection and control were enacted and discussed. Following one of the dyadic sessions in this period father said to the therapist: 'It is clear to me now that my parents should have sent me to therapy, if they had really understood me.' There was pain and revelation, and maybe also unconscious envy of what was given to Adam by his father but not given to father himself. By reflecting on the meaning of their parent–child relationship, in the accepting and supporting atmosphere of the sessions, father was able and willing to recognize his parental role. The child's needs triggered and kindled an important developmental process for both of them. Getting in touch with his own deprivation enabled father to feel happy for Adam, and also for his own 'child within' that was now receiving, through Adam's treatment, some delayed 'reparation'.

In the last sessions, Adam mostly tested whether father was available; listening and following him, rather than being intrusive. They were both learning to be alone in the presence of the other while feeling satisfied and secure.

In the mother–child dyad, the image of the mother is that of someone trying to supply everything all the time for her son, providing immediate fulfilment for all his needs. Mother used the dyadic sessions to learn new ways of communicating with Adam together with more developmentally helpful forms of interaction, sometimes even on a procedural level.

In the first sessions their interactions were quite calm. Gradually, the sessions became stormier. With hindsight the change started as a reaction to the improvement in Adam's relationship with his father. Mother had difficulty in giving up the special relationship she had had with her son, which excluded the father as the 'bad one' and which also compensated for her bad marital relationship. Mother needed much help in lessening her inhibition of self-expression, spontaneity and assertiveness as a caregiver in her current relations with Adam.

Adam became gradually more and more aggressive towards his mother, who was ready to accept a lot of his abusive behaviour before she reacted. While trying hard to 'supply' him narcissistically and also to control his anger, she became easily tired, withdrawn and often left him by himself. When their regressive togetherness was not satisfying any more, they both felt 'abandoned'. Adam's saying 'I am bored' was understood by mother as expressing his feelings of self-depletion and self-devaluation. Mother almost always interpreted it as her failure and tried desperately to repair it. She could not bear his aggressiveness, or his anxiety. Her efforts to regulate him were unclear and inappropriate for the strength of his affects. Adam's feelings of emptiness and boredom were so threatening to mother that she tried immediately to 'do' something about them. Her mothering style did not enable Adam to identify and understand well enough his own emotions, or to get control over them. Finding meaningful support in the therapist's approach and a kind of 'developmental psychoeducation', mother was able to lessen her inhibition of self-expression and to renew her efforts to control Adam's anxiety, but her unclear messages – of being together through 'doing', instead of attuning to him – delayed the boy's process of differentiation and self-expression. As treatment proceeded, Adam permitted himself to scream at her: 'leave me alone, let me go'. But when she complied with his request, with the slightest frustration, he would scream again: 'it's all your fault'. Mother and Adam were struggling to separate from their maladaptive relations.

In the sessions the therapist had with both parents, mother started to express her anger, and how tired it made her to be an omnipotent object for Adam. Her functioning as a self-object for her own mother was discussed and better understood. She was helped to see that letting Adam be more autonomous was not equivalent to losing him or abandoning him.

In the sessions before the end of the treatment, instead of going to the toilet or screaming 'I am bored', Adam was able to tell his parents: 'Something is happening inside me, I don't know what it is and I don't know how to stop it.' He was aware of the need for self-regulation that was verbalized and communicated to his parents. The ability to reflect on internal states, to verbalize, and to communicate about them was an achievement for everyone in the family. Adam's turning to his parents when he became aware of his inner turmoil expressed the establishment of proper family roles for parents and child.

The family situation today

Adam adjusted well to school. He is a very good student and has satisfying relations with his peers. The marital relationship is very much improved, even though it was not an explicit focus of the treatment process. Now the mother can see the father as a helping figure and father can accept his wife's criticism of his behaviour with Adam. They can support each other better and find in their relationship some fulfilment of their needs instead of projecting them on to the child. Mother is now pregnant with their second child. They feel more confident and stronger, both as a couple and as parents. The family unit is more differentiated and also more united.

Chapter 10

A short dyadic treatment

Therapist: Y. Ronen

Berry, an 8-year-old boy, participated in dyadic treatment that lasted nine months. He was seen alternately with his mother in 16 dyadic meetings, and with his father in 15. In addition, each of the parents was seen individually by the same therapist (seven meetings with the mother and five meetings with the father), a set-up preferred by both parents, suitable for the therapeutic needs of the child.

Berry was referred to the clinic by his parents at their own initiative. They were concerned, especially the mother, with Berry's recurrent complaints about stomach aches before leaving for school and about his extreme dependence on help from her in every area of daily life in any of the most simple activities, such as dressing. From the short assessment period, the therapist learned that, together with the extreme dependence and inhibition of initiative on Berry's part, there were also endless quarrels, almost exclusively with mother, that lured him into agreeing with and opposing at the same time any of her points of view. The therapist was struck by the boy's clumsy movements and incomprehensible speech (which his parents were also unable to understand) at their meetings. Recent medical examinations had found nothing wrong. Mother was unusually involved with the boy's undefined 'problems'. They were felt by her to be due to her own inadequacy, and she wanted to get help. The father was a quiet and rather withdrawn man. Berry's 6-year-old sister was described as a much easier child to raise. In school Berry was slow to learn and passive with other children.

The intake process

During the first two months of treatment, a recurrent pattern of interaction was observed in both dyads. With the mother, this consisted mostly of conversations turning into quarrels. With the father, a different characteristic pattern emerged of physical interactions, such as ball games.

Mother

The mother would constantly criticize and devalue whatever Berry was saying, feeling or doing about any subject. She would force him into a submissive role of thinking and acting as she expected, and when he accepted her point of view and followed it, mother, as if disappointed, would contradict him. Berry was desperately trying to please his mother, and at the same time would argue with her quite aggressively. The impression that the mother gave, of inviting and supporting the boy's aggressive quarrelling with the implicit aim of controlling it, was confirmed in her individual meetings with the therapist.

The mother was the eldest daughter in her family. By her own account, she had been seen as 'inadequate and very disappointing' by her parents, who had been extremely 'critical and disparaging' of her views and actions. She recalled vividly her painful helplessness, and declared that she had 'to do anything to spare Berry this kind of pain'. Even now, Berry's difficulty in making decisions made her suffer, as if happening to her. Mother saw the quarrelling with Berry as a way of 'being with him as a mother' and helping him to be 'as he should be'. In the individual meetings with mother the therapist tried to help her, in a kind of psycho-education, to define and revalidate the meanings of the role of a parent and the role of a child in her interaction with Berry. There was also discussion of the differing needs and opposing wishes, both in the present and in the past. In the safety provided by the set-up, the mother was able quite soon to confront her fears of the boy's aggression, as well as her own anger evoked by his feelings of helplessness.

Father

The father, a warm, quite dull person very dependent on mother, was a local football coach. He found much pleasure in this position. Father gave little information about his past history and present family life. In individual meetings, he was helped to look at parental roles through focusing on his coaching, its aims and duties. In the father–child dyadic meetings the interaction was divided from the beginning into two parts. The boy had to work quite hard to engage his withdrawn father's attention, but when he succeeded, as usually happened, they spent the second part of the meetings in mutually satisfying ball games.

Treatment

The main themes that Berry brought up with both parents, but especially with mother, were: How can we be together and yet remain different? And:

I want to be different but am afraid, because being different means being alone. These themes became more explicit with the help of the therapist who, through verbalization and mirroring, acted as a translator of the boy's needs, feeling and fears.

After three months of treatment there was a visible change in the interaction of Berry with each of his parents. An excerpt from the 9th dyadic session with mother illustrates it.

> Mother: 'Berry, you wanted to tell the therapist something.'
> Berry: 'Oh. Yes, I got two fish.'
> Therapist: 'Are these the fish you were talking about last time we met? The fish you were planning to buy?'
> Berry: 'I was not planning. I decided to buy it.' (The boy looks pleased with himself. He smiles and seems quite assertive).
> Mother (in a condescending tone): 'That's the problem with Berry. For him things cannot remain plans or dreams. He needs to turn them into reality at once.'
> Berry (tries to catch the therapist's attention): 'You know, one of the fish gave birth to two small ones, but one of them disappeared.'
> Therapist: 'Disappeared?'
> Mother (has an annoyed facial expression). 'Yes, but they are so small. Who knows, maybe they jumped out, or maybe they were swallowed.'
> Therapist: 'It seems that Berry is happy with the fish and it is not clear how mother feels about them?'
> Mother: 'No I'm happy. An aquarium is a wonderful thing. It's just that Berry [in a complaining voice] always wants everything at once, and this is a problem. For instance, we bought the aquarium and then we found out that it needs an air pump. Berry convinced his father to go and buy one immediately. When they came back they found out it did not fit. So, we spent money and what's going to happen now?'
> Berry: 'We will buy a new one.'

Berry and mother went into a long argument. They both got more and more annoyed with each other but could not seem to find a way out. Mother's role in the interaction was to negate Berry's wishes. There was a strong impression that the mother was compelled to criticize – no matter whom, the child or herself.

In the session Berry tried to say to mother: 'I need you to accept me as I am, and to see in me someone you can accept.' At this point he felt safe arguing with his mother while she criticized him. It seemed that there was already a different feeling for Berry in the way he argued with his mother. He now did not just lure her into arguments, which was a familiar way for both of them to be together, but expressed his wishes in a more assertive way and was persistent on what was important to him; for instance, his aquarium.

At the following meeting between the therapist and the mother she gave a long list of Berry's characteristics in which 'he was exactly like her, therefore suffering in life'. To the question whether there were some attributes in which Berry and mother differed, she replied by adding a few differences then stopped and said, 'No, actually we aren't different at all.'

Two sessions later Berry started in a playful way to tell his mother about the results of his rough play (ball games, dart throwing) with father, after finding in the room some signs of this that remained from their previous session. Jokingly he told her that they had decided to call the damage they had caused to the plants in the therapy room – the many fallen leaves – 'autumn in the room'. At first mother seemed intimidated and almost shocked by Berry's storm, but rather quickly Berry and mother engaged in a ball game that soon turned out to be rough. They seemed very involved with the game and with each other when suddenly Berry shouted, 'So, who do you think I am?'. Mother looked at him and said, 'You are someone strong, maybe even someone to be afraid of.'

In the following dyadic session mother and Berry went back almost immediately to the rough ball game, treating it both seriously and playfully at the same time. One session later, when Berry told his mother about some 'water bombs' he had made at school, mother excitedly started planning all the nasty things he could do with them. At this point Berry changed the subject, as if saying that, after all, it was his invention and his boldness, and that mother seemed to be going too far in using it for her own needs.

These sessions were a turning point in Berry's and mother's relationship.

During the same period, in the dyadic meetings with father, it took Berry less effort and time than before to establish communication with his withdrawn father, and they spent most of their time playing ball games, and talking about games that father coached. Berry even permitted himself to advise and to criticize his father's decisions as a coach. The atmosphere was pleasant, father seemed to enjoy Berry's ideas and argued with him like a peer. Father's attitude – his acceptance of the boy's views as valid and their joyful exchange – was a major support for Berry's developmental changes. The recurrent experience that, after cueing his father and waiting patiently, his father would respond, assured the boy that he was important, a 'somebody', and led to many positive feelings. Their joy and the appreciation they showed each other was put into words by the therapist.

It is important to stress that Berry, who was described as a clumsy boy, and did usually behave that way when with mother, responded adequately to father's expectations of performance in ball games. His posture and movements became appropriate for his age. He probably needed his father's admiration and reflection in order to experience himself as somebody who was capable of this.

In the parallel sessions with the mother they seemed to be busy learning to know each other in their new roles. At times mother moved into Berry's role, joining as his equal in the rough play, or even initiating it. At times Berry would imitate mother's role in planning, for example, a family Sunday trip to see the trees in blossom.

Satisfied by a new mutuality as well as by a better defined separateness, Berry and mother, with empathic help from the therapist, learned to express their pleasure in their differences as well as in their similarities. Soon enough Berry, reassured by her genuine acceptance, conveyed to his mother assertively his needs from her and of her, thus prompting in the mother feelings of competence in her maternal role.

In the sequence of the therapeutic sessions, themes from meetings with mother were continued in meetings with father and vice versa. In this way the child was building up his self-evaluation through the comparison between his mother's and father's reactions, and their complementarity. It was obvious that Berry's interactions with father enabled the child to increase his assertive behaviour with the mother. The father's pleasurable participation, as conveyed through the child's play, also helped the mother to contain her strong ambivalence towards rough activities. For mother, it is probable that a sense of the father's presence as the 'third one' in the room was helpful in letting her become more assertive, as was the therapist's communication that there are safe barriers to aggressive and hostile wishes.

At the end of the therapy the change in mother's and Berry's relations seemed well established. Mother was content both with her motherhood and with Berry's behaviour. She felt the change and described it as a 'new mood' between herself and the rest of the family.

The change in Berry could also be seen in his movements and his speech. He was free of previously troublesome pain symptoms. His relationship with his mother was stable and generally positive. In the last therapy session Berry asked his mother to sit by him. He gave her a big chunk of play dough and asked her to prepare bits of the material for him by warming them in her hands. He then built from the bits mother gave to him a happy looking warrior, to the excitement and delight of both of them, and decided, with mother's consent, to take the 'warrior' home.

CHAPTER 11

A girl suffering from chronic constipation

Therapist: T. Shacher

Sue was referred for treatment by her nursery teacher at the age of 2 years and 7 months because of 'emotional problems'. She was described as very quiet and passive, uninvolved with other children. 'One couldn't tell if she was there or not.' She was noticed only when the children moved from one activity to another – then she would cry, always saying 'I have poo... I have poo'.

The intake process

Sue was the youngest of four children, all of whom suffered from untreated psychological difficulties. Her father, the eldest of three children, had been a technical worker, but following a car accident he was unemployed. Confined to a wheelchair he was unable to leave the house. The mother worked in a factory, and took care of her husband. She came from a poor and large family of 13 children. Her parents had divorced when she was a child, after which she was sent to a boarding school. In spite of the many family difficulties, mother says that she never had any negative feelings towards her parents. She felt only love and respect, and always tried to be 'a good daughter, responding to their needs'. In her youth, she worked in a nursing home for the elderly. At the time of Sue's assessment, mother was very successful in her work, always smiling: 'everything is in perfect order and under control'.

Mother described Sue as a very easy baby, who did not ask 'to be held'. Their relationship was focused on breast feeding, nappy changing and sleeping together while Sue clung to her mother's body.

When Sue was one and a half years old, mother had stopped breast feeding her, following father's car accident. Two months later Sue had developed severe constipation with attacks of abdominal pain. At each attack, mother would stop her other activities, and dedicate herself totally to Sue – hugging and massaging her, pressing and caressing her tummy. After a while, mother would declare: 'That's enough! Now we are going to do some poo!' Then mother folded Sue's legs, pressed her tummy, and finally pressed her anus until she had a bowel movement. During all these procedures, Sue was screaming and crying. Mother says, 'these episodes were like giving birth, contractions, pain, bleeding and all'. Although the symptoms were severe, the parents had not asked for treatment until they were referred by the nursery teacher. The dyad was seen every week, and the mother every second week. It had been agreed that father would join the therapy as soon as possible, but since he was not rehabilitated until the last months of treatment, this did not materialize.

Dyadic psychotherapy was the preferred mode of treatment for practical and theoretical reasons: mother and Sue were not separate enough, and there was a sense of emergency because of the persistent symptoms and Sue's arrested development. Mother seemed to be lacking reflective capacity and symbolic ability and the most efficient mode of learning for her was through direct experience.

The following vignettes from the first two months of therapy (Sue aged 2 years and 7 months) demonstrate the psychosomatic partnership of Sue and mother, and the first signs of Sue's 'hatching' from this 'oneness' that was so inappropriate for her age, and was limiting her development. The restricted range of verbal and other symbolic interaction was prominent, and the therapist helped by reflecting on mother's and Sue's internal states, labelling them and promoting differentiation between them. She was creating an atmosphere of safety, both in a concrete way (giving aprons to mother and Sue, when they were painting) and emotionally (in the supportive stance to mother), in order to encourage self- and other reflection in both participants, and enable Sue's development to proceed.

Treatment

First month

Mother and Sue are in the waiting room, Sue curled up in mother's arms like a baby, bottle in one hand and a curl of mother's hair in the other. As soon as they enter the therapy room, mother says to Sue: 'go ahead and do something'. Sue sticks to mother, she is very quiet, looks at the toys with no expression on her face.

> Therapist: 'It seems to me that mother would like Sue to play immediately, but maybe she needs some time near you at the beginning.'

Mother touches Sue's back and says: 'Look! There on the floor, there are some nice toys.' Sue moves slowly to the toys mother pointed out to her, and sluggishly picks up a phone and brings it to mother.

> Mother: 'You can call Daddy!'

Sue puts the phone to her ear. Mother says: 'not like that, hold it here. Put your finger here and do it like this; it will be easier, and you can also do it sitting.' After manipulating Sue's hands she lifts her and seats her in a small chair, then pushes the chair closer to the table.

> Therapist: 'I can see, mother, how important it is for you to help Sue and make things easy for her, even things she can do by herself.'

Second month

Mother decides that Sue should draw. Sue puts the crayons and paper on the floor ready to draw. Mother takes the crayons and paper, without any warning or explanation, and puts them on the table. Mother picks up Sue and seats her by the table, then sits down herself waiting for Sue to draw. Sue sits looking confused and sad and does nothing.

> Therapist: 'It looks like mother wanted to help you, but you wanted to draw on the floor and now you don't want to draw anymore.
> Sue (in a whining voice): 'Bottle, bottle.'
> Mother: 'No, later...in the car.'
> Therapist: 'You would prefer it now but mother thinks it better for you to have it in the car.'

Sue gets up from the chair, goes to mother's handbag and takes out her bottle. She walks around the room with the bottle hanging from her mouth.

> Mother, in a worried tone: 'You can't walk like this, you might fall, come sit on my lap.'

Sue continues her walk and lifts the bottle higher to drink while walking. Suddenly she staggers and mother jumps up from her chair, embraces her and sits down with her in her arms. Sue lies there holding mother's curl and her bottle.

> Therapist: 'You tried to do as you chose and it was nice, and now it is nice to be held by mother.'

From these dyadic sessions, and from the sessions with mother, it was understood that mother's behaviour had two aspects. She had to feel needed and vital to Sue (maybe because when she was not needed by her own parents she had been sent away), and she had to control her. Sue probably experienced mother as very intrusive, leaving no room for her own initiatives to develop. Sue had to mould herself to mother's intentions and developed a 'false self' to keep their relations going. The dependence on her mother was given additional importance by her father's absence from Sue's life. Mother could not tolerate any negative feelings or the slightest discomfort in Sue, because these might damage her image of herself as the 'perfect mother'. These motives were also present in her marital relationship. The therapist held this image of mother in her mind, and tried to make both mother and Sue aware of it in order to help them to know and better understand each other.

Mother's coping and defences against negative emotions are demonstrated in the following vignettes, as well as the process of Sue's regulation of negative affect. Sue by now, expresses anger in a clearer way, but also identifies with mother's reaction to sadness and pain. The therapist stresses the different ways of coping with different affects.

Eight months into therapy

Mother takes a bite from one of three cookies on a plate. Sue screams loudly. Mother puts the cookie back and says: 'Take them all, you eat them all.' Sue continues screaming.

> Therapist: 'You look really angry.'
> Mother: 'I will buy you a whole bag of cookies, just for you! Come here, I will hug you!'

Sue is still screaming. Mother takes Sue in her arms; dances with her around the room; sings to her; tells her funny things and when all these do not help she starts to tickle her. Sue laughs and mother sits down exhausted. As soon as they are sitting, Sue screams again.

> Therapist: 'Sometimes children are angry and adults are angry too. It takes time to calm down. I can see that you, mother, would do anything to help Sue be happy but sometimes we cannot and maybe should not influence each other's feelings.'

Mother listens to the therapist, then suggests some playdough to Sue, who leaves her mother's lap and goes to the playdough and kicks it angrily.

Therapist: 'It looks like Sue wants to show us that she is still angry.'

After a while Sue takes some blocks and builds a tower. As she adds one more block the tower falls. Mother laughs. Sue starts again, but again the tower falls. Mother laughs and collects the blocks for Sue, who looks sad, her head lowered to her chest, as if sinking into herself.

Therapist: 'You look so sad, your body is collapsing as the tower did. Maybe mother thinks that it is not so sad and you can build it again?'

Sue gets up, goes to the shelves and looks into a big box with different masks. She chooses one and when she raises her head she hits it on the shelf. It is a hard knock, sounding loudly in the room. Mother laughs loudly and so does Sue, with a kitty's mask on her face.

The therapist feels amazed and says: 'I thought it hurts but it looks like you and mother find it funny! You laugh like mother.'

In the domain of negative affects there was no 'interpersonal communion' between mother and Sue, so Sue learned that they could not be shared with mother. In the sessions with mother alone, the different meanings of negative affect were explored and different ways of coping were discussed. Since mother never expressed any negative affect in her sessions with the therapist regarding her past or present relationships, the dyadic sessions were the only source of knowing about them and experiencing them in safety.

Sue used the dyadic sessions to experiment with negative affects towards the therapist instead of mother.

Ten months into therapy

Mother and the therapist are talking to each other. Sue takes a toy gun and shoots.

Therapist: 'Maybe you are angry at us because we were not talking to you too?'
Sue: 'But I am shooting only at you!'
Therapist: 'I understand that you do not want to hurt mother.'
Sue goes closer to the therapist and whispers to her: 'I hurt mother at home when I don't make poo for her.'

She also practised separation and abandonment with the therapist first, and only later with mother.

Eleven months into therapy

Sue plays her ritual game of hide-and-seek that has evolved in this period. Mother and Sue hide in a closet together. The therapist searches for them, expressing her feelings (I miss them, I hope they didn't leave me because they were angry with me, I don't like being alone, etc.). Then mother and Sue emerge happily from the closet. In the second phase of the game the therapist hides in the closet and mother and Sue look for her. Mother says similar things to what the therapist said before, only this time, after she is found, Sue dares to ask mother to hide in the closet. The therapist and Sue look for mother but when they open the closet, to their great surprise, mother is not there. She is in the room and Sue runs to her. Mother runs away and a game of chasing mother develops. Mother and Sue are laughing.

> Therapist: 'It was a surprise not to find mother, maybe it was even a little frightening. You wanted mother to wait for you in the closet, but maybe mother felt sad alone in there and that's why she left.'

Mother identifies with the therapist, and learns something more about caring as a mother. She also identifies with the 'abandoned child' within her. The roles shift in this game between leaving and being left. Thus, the game can proceed, although the affects aroused are difficult.

The following vignette demonstrates the progress Sue was making in expression through symbolic play, in spite of mother's difficulty with this mode of relating.

Twenty months into therapy – age 4 years 3 months

Sue plays with her stuffed kitten she has brought from home; she feeds it, takes it for a walk and then on a visit to the Barbie doll's house. She takes a small toy bottle and asks all the guests: 'Who wants orange juice?'

> Mother: 'You know I am not allowed to have citrus juice!'

Sue gives her 'banana juice'.

The final phase

The therapy is now in the ending phase, after about two years. Sue's functioning in the nursery improved fairly quickly. After 18 months of treatment she became a dominant figure in the nursery, a 'leader'. She has many friends. She is very talkative, and about varied subjects. She is creative and happy. The teachers have described some difficulties in setting limits for her. The situation at home changed slowly, but in the last six months of therapy the constipation stopped altogether. Father was able to move more freely and to get out. He became very important to Sue, especially as someone who sets limits for the children. Sue is very independent at home. She is assertive with mother, but their confrontations are mostly verbal. She does not scream when mother refuses her wishes. Mother tries to please her most of the time and leaves the discipline to father.

Discussion

Cases like this are frequently encountered in the population of children considered to be at risk for developmental problems. The therapeutic process in this particular case took longer, mostly because of the mother's inhibitions and limited emotional resources, and because of the therapist's lack of experience with this form of therapy.

The case demonstrates the learning process of a mother with a restricted emotional and mental life, a 'doer', who was nevertheless very dedicated to her child. Mother moved from being totally 'at one' with the child to differentiating and regarding her as a separate psychological being. It was interesting to note that mental separation was easier for mother than physical separation, and it took her a long time to give up her child's body as a domain that should be regulated and manipulated by her to perform basic physiological functions. The dyadic format enabled both mother and Sue to experience the two different meanings of mother's behaviour: the perfect, helpful mother and the intrusive mother. A more suitable balance was achieved between these two aspects, better suited to Sue's developmental needs. In the dyadic sessions, the therapist's labelling and acknowledging of Sue's feelings helped mother to focus on and enrich her inner life. It became better understood and less threatening, although these changes were limited.

In the framework of working alliance and the positive transference to the therapist, mother could identify and internalize some of the helpful attitudes to the child. An approach of watching and trying to work out the possible meanings of Sue's behaviour, in terms of intentions, was adopted as the best way of providing psychoeducation for the mother and supporting her reflective functioning. Mother was attuned to the child's needs and participated in her experiences, but had difficulty in giving them meaning that her daughter could use as a way of thinking of herself and of her feelings as meaningful to others and to herself. The child, supported by the development-promoting experiences in the dyadic meetings, was able to find in her playful relations with the father, and in her interactions with the nursery school teachers and her peers, a necessary additional environment for shared experiences that contributed to her sense of self-agency and self-regulation.

CHAPTER 12

'A name is given'

Therapist: D. Glat

Nel, a girl of 4 years and 10 months, was referred for treatment by her parents on the insistence of her nursery school teacher who described her 'as a very lonely child, pushing off any invitation from other children to play together and keeping her distance from the teachers'. The girl's mother was described as having great difficulty separating from Nel 'as though nobody can be trusted to take care of the child'. The parents complained in their application about Nel's slowness, even clumsiness, extreme caution, restriction of movements and lack of initiative. The family had moved from the city to an agricultural settlement (kibbutz), a year previously, because of economic difficulties. The father, an engineer, found work in the kibbutz as a mechanic, and the mother as a professional caretaker of elderly people. There was another child in the family, a boy, a year and a half old.

The intake process

The assessment of Nel consisted of two meetings with the two parents, two alternating meetings with the mother–child and father–child dyads, and a diagnostic meeting with the girl. In the first session mother, the main speaker (father seemed to feel very uncomfortable) reported almost immediately that at the age of 8 months Nel had been diagnosed as suffering from cancer. Until the age of 2 years she had frequently been hospitalized and had undergone chemotherapy. At referral, she continued follow-up tests every six months, but was considered 'out of danger and with no health problems'. Mother gave the information in a very matter-of-fact way without any affect, details or personal recollections – as if something dreadful had happened but it did not belong to her. In the beginning phase of treatment, whenever mother talked about the subject she described mostly her battles to obtain adequate treatment for her baby, who was not correctly diagnosed; only mother's insistence had 'saved the child at the last minute'. It was quite obvious that 'the illness' was invested with strong ambivalent affects and it was not clear to the therapist to which body – the girl's or the mother's – it 'belonged'.

At the age of 2 years Nel had been placed in a nursery and adjusted well there. Both parents stressed that her development, in spite of the treatments, had been good. She was a cheerful, friendly and curious girl. For the parents, the period before their forced move to the kibbutz had been 'a happy one, with a lot of supporting friends', very different from their 'present hardship'. Both parent gave no additional information about themselves, separating past from the present.

In the dyadic meeting with father (he had the first of these meetings, by choice), as well as with mother, Nel played by herself and kept to the same themes. One of them was a doll travelling in a car. When asked by the therapist she explained that 'the doll is sick and is taken by an ambulance to hospital'. Father sat at a distance, quite detached, and the girl addressed the therapist who, while verbally following Nel's play, informed her that she knew from the parents about the child's hospitalization as a baby. Nel continued to play with a few dolls and talked to the therapist about what they were doing. In any normally social games, such as cards or dominoes, she preferred to play by herself.

The therapist asked father how he had explained to Nel the purpose of the dyadic meeting and father said 'Nel needs help because she has no friends' and added that 'it is probably hard for Nel and it is hard for her parents'. In response Nel took a pony doll and told the therapist that 'the pony has a horse-friend in grandpa's kibbutz' (this is not the one that the family lives in). She continued, 'the pony is small and cannot fight back when others do things to him by force, and the people meant to look after him do not take proper care of him'. The therapist verbalized her understanding of what Nel said about being small and unable to deal with stress alone. Nel seemed to be pleased with this kind of dialogue. After some encouragement father joined Nel, but started to build from Lego pieces mostly for his own enjoyment, and Nel ended the short period of playing with him.

In the meeting with father the child showed not only readiness but a need to tell her story, and seemed to make the conversation through play quite easy to understand. Father tried to be 'present' but was quite reluctant in joining the child in what was relevant to her. It seemed that father was willing but needed help to find out how he could give Nel a feeling of parental support and care.

In the meeting with mother, Nel repeated the sequence and the themes in her play although she seemed to expect more direction from mother.

She played and talked like a younger child. Mother did not verbalize the stories Nel played out, neither did she join in when the therapist spoke about them. It seemed that the themes were felt by her to be dangerous. Instead mother tried, quite forcefully, to change the mood of Nel's stories – it was 'great fun to drive in the car' when commenting on Nel's playing driving to a hospital, for example. Mother was observing the child's play but refused to connect and understand Nel's intentions and implicit meanings.

From the interview and a battery of tests we learned that Nel was a very bright child with good verbal skills of which she was not making full use, she seemed confused about her body image and overwhelmed by feelings of helplessness and abandonment. She looked and behaved like a small, vulnerable child, more like a 3-year-old than a 5-year-old. There was something mechanical and doll-like about her appearance and contact with others – as if things were just done, not talked about or thought about.

In the review session with both parents, it seemed that the move to a new place had been traumatic to both the parents and the child. The circumstance – the father's failure to provide material security and the change from a supporting atmosphere to the not very friendly relations in the kibbutz – had undermined the already shaky equilibrium between the parents, as providers and caregivers, and their child. It was obvious that the severe illness in her childhood had left the parents and the child in a state of painful and frightening confusion. It was observed that Nel used bodily sensations, manipulation of toys, objects and her own body as the main domain of self-expression. She needed and looked for adequate verbalization of what was going on, and explanations, that neither parent was providing. She expressed her feelings of insecurity, and even danger, by her cautiousness, and almost constant preoccupation with the same traumatic experiences.

Mother conveyed to the child her feeling that nobody could be trusted; even mother could not help her (e.g. mother's difficulty in leaving Nel in the nursery school), and at the same time denied any problems. She was reported to have told Nel once or twice that she had been hospitalized as a baby but did not give any explanations to the girl. It was not a subject to be talked about and whenever Nel 'asked in play' mother reacted to it as the 'ordinary play of a child'. Mother, at this stage, was unable to relate empathically to the idea of a sick girl. She had to split the illness, equated with badness, and her child. Father, as was confirmed later, had seemed to be almost paralysed by the child's severe state and left mother to cope alone with their sick daughter.

The parents and the child needed and were asking for help. The therapist suggested dyadic treatment. Mother was pleased and relieved by the fact that she would be an active partner in the help given to the child. The therapist at this stage was quite sure that mother would participate in the therapeutic process in many roles and not only as caregiver. Weekly alternate meetings with each dyad were decided on, and bi-weekly sessions with the mother–father dyad, with the same therapist.

Treatment

Nel's treatment continued for 15 months.

The beginning phase

During the first three months both parents and Nel 'learned' their respective roles in the meetings: the parents learned their role as collaborators in the treatment effort, with Nel as the main theme presenter, while the therapist acted as a translator and narrator. Nel would usually play by herself, and the parent would observe her in silence. When the theme seemed neutral to the father he tried to join Nel by verbally guiding her from a distance – he called it 'teaching'. Mother would closely watch Nel's play but would engage the therapist in her associations and was obviously avoiding any allusions to illness or pain.

The child was, most of the time and in every possible way, playing out questions about danger, failure, getting help or helplessness. In one session when father 'taught' her how to play a table football game she refused to do it his way and chose to play alone. She took two balls and played with them. Asked by the therapist what she was telling them by her play, she called one of the balls 'a dumped, dead ball', then put the other ball nearby and declared 'when this one joins the other they are both alive'. Father was annoyed with Nel and said 'you are inventing rules of your own and not accepting the usual one'. The therapist described the child's play as posing a question about what makes things or people feel bad and what makes them feel good and alive. Father withdrew from interaction and almost fell asleep. The therapist engaged father and the child and discussed with them the sensation of extreme tiredness to help father be aware of his defensive reactions to Nel's difficulties and to lessen the child's feelings that she was alone.

In this phase the main work concerning the child's pressing questions about her illness, now and in the past, was done in the meetings with mother. From the dyadic sessions, as well as the meetings with the two parents, it could be understood that for mother the sick child and/or illness represented a devalued 'bad' part of herself. Mother, an only child of elderly parents (she is now a professional caretaker of adults), born in a kibbutz (not the one that she now lives in), felt rejected and very lonely in her age group, her main link with 'home'. She had been in psychotherapy as a child (at 8 to 10 years old) because of her 'badness'. Only when she left the kibbutz as a young adult did she 'find herself'. Her husband abandoned her to many hardships and left her, almost alone, with the apparently dying child. The feeling that she had to suffer did not leave her for a long time. Nel quite soon projected on to the therapist her own or her mother's 'badness' and called her 'the witch'.

In the meetings with mother, repeating the sequences from the meetings with father, Nel enacted themes of physical pain, intrusions by injections and treatments, feelings of despair and loneliness. Quite unusually, Nel expressed her wishes and needs to mother and father in a general way, for instance 'there is a need for this doll...' instead of 'I need...'. The therapist focused mother's attention on the fact that Nel was not asking directly, but stated what was needed. Requests for help and expectations of getting help were discussed in the meetings and mother started to wonder about this, and began to find out how to understand the child better.

At the end of this period Nel directly invited 'the witch-therapist' to play with her on the theme of a 'sick doll that is taken to the hospital'. Mother needed the active support of the therapist and requests from the child before she would participate in the play. Nel gave injections to the doll and the therapist and manipulated the doll in a way that seemed like an actualization of her memories of the many treatments that she had received. The setting of the meetings, the active participation of the therapist and the presence of the parents helped Nel to establish a more secure feeling, a safer boundary between herself and the mother, thus enabling her to work on the most important theme for her. Both her parents used disavowal of affect regarding the child's state and defended themselves by 'not understanding' any symbolization of her experiences, as represented in play.

The middle phase

During the next eight months Nel was actively engaged in remembering what had happened to her and acting out her 'badness'. Mother, who was now ready to participate in the verbalization of Nel's different experiences, had to have help to free her inhibited ability to attune herself to and reflect on the girl's mental state. Nel started to be a naughty, angry and fighting girl, used 'dirty words', and damaged many objects at home and in the room used for therapy.

At almost every session with mother, Nel was busy giving injections and treatments to a few regular dolls. Prompted by the therapist, mother explained each time about the relevant current follow-up tests and previous treatments at the hospital. Nel listened very attentively to mother's words. In one session she suddenly asked 'why was I sick, mother?'. In reaction to mother's answer 'I do not know' Nel started to shout in anger. The therapist tried to lessen mother's feelings of fright and supported her in giving simple, clear explanations of how one gets sick, how the body fights, what help is needed, etc., serious answers appropriate for a 5-year-old girl. The child seemed greatly relieved that mother knew what was happening to her and her body.

Nel was using the dolls and quite often the witch-therapist's arm to apply different treatments – injections, radiation and so on. In some sessions she played out a CT scan (a recollection from two and a half years old), and mother explained to her what it was for. Nel showed some lesions on her legs, and a lesion on her chest. The child was learning about the 'damages' and the 'repairs' that had been done to her body. Securely embedded in her mother's emotional availability, Nel played out her questions and received answers from a 'helping mother'. The therapist was needed to formulate, translate and bridge the pieces of sensation, the feelings and recollections of the child, and the mother's efforts to deal with her own pain in order to be sufficiently available to Nel.

In one of the sessions Nel used, for the first time according to the very surprised mother, the word 'cancer', a word that had never been directly mentioned to her, as if saying 'now I can give a name to the terrifying feelings'. Nel even told her mother about somebody who had died of cancer, in their now frequent discussions of 'serious' matters which continued at home. In another session Nel asked the therapist if she had seen a 'dog jumping on another dog'. The therapist explained that the animals were copulating. Nel took down from the shelf an illustrated book entitled *This is Not a Secret* and asked mother to read it to her. Quite quickly resolving her conflicting feelings, mother read the book to Nel.

Nel now more secure about her own body, gave expression to her natural curiosity about her mother's body, the relations between her parents, her baby brother, etc. Mother reported that there was a remarkable change in Nel's contact with other children and participation in what was going on at home and in the nursery school. At the same time Nel started to be very provocative in the consulting room as well as at home, as if testing the different expressions of anger and resistance, and her parents' possible reactions to her behaviour. She had to build with them the experiential meaning of punishment, restrictions and containment.

Discussions with the parents in their dyadic meetings helped them understand Nel's many needs, expressed in her provocative assertiveness and tests of autonomy, as well as in her anger about what was done to her body. The parents brought to the session some photos taken in the hospital of Nel on her second birthday in the company of the treating physicians and nurses, symbolically 'completing' the picture of the girl.

In the meetings with the father Nel started to play competitive games with him, after she asked for and received an explanation from the therapist of what competition means. Father was very pleased with Nel's 'liveliness' and was quite adequate in dealing with her new adaptive and maladaptive demands. Having withdrawn from the 'mortally sick girl' he found much reassurance in her 'fighting stance'. This could also be noticed in his dealings with outside problems and in his relations with the mother. As he said, the girl had injected him with hope. Father appreciated Nel's demands to do everything by herself, even if it was difficult for her. For example, although afraid, she would climb a high gym ladder and refused to be helped down. Father directed her descent by 'verbally moving' her legs and both felt pride and satisfaction.

Although it was harder for mother to accept Nel's opposition and separation, she was more aware of her own conflicting needs as well as those of the child, and was able to reflect on them. She was trying to help in every possible way Nel's learning in the present about her past. The child needed not only to talk, but to relive it experientially in the context of relations with the present mother and father. It was an effort for mother to build up new relations with a contemporary Nel who had changed their respective role relations quite drastically. Nel needed an accepting mother who would help and support a sick child, but not be afraid of her 'badness' and not be awaiting punishment. Mother found support in father, in her identification with the helping but not omnipotent stance of the therapist and, most of all, in the validation by the child and the therapist of her unique role as a good-enough mother.

The ending phase

After almost a year of treatment, the last five months were spent in reading books. Nel chose some from the small library in the consulting room and asked (a remarkable change for her), both parents to read to her continuously from the same book, at each consecutive meeting. She chose a book about a witch who took care of a boy and about a girl who was afraid and cried at night. Nel would usually sit with a doll near the parent who read, and enacted the narration and interactions in the story by movements and emotional expressions.

It was a kind of actualization of the themes, and integration between the word of the parent and the experiencing through action of the child. Most remarkably, Nel found a book (with illustrations) of a crippled girl entitled *I Shall Overcome*. For almost three months each parent and Nel were absorbed by the well-written story. Nel stopped the reading sessions with the protagonist's entering school (Nel was to enter first grade soon). The story centred on the pain, despair and the anger of the girl who was unable to walk in spite of many operations, on the feelings of her parents, their fears and concerns about the future, the girl's confrontations with other children and so on. Nel asked questions about the girl in the book, and about herself. The parents, especially the mother, with the therapist's help, described to Nel what had happened to them, comparing and using the expressions from the book to convey their own feelings and memories. With the help of this book mother and Nel co-constructed the child's new and full biography. Nel was building up her self-understanding through sensorimotor experiences, sharing them with each parent and learning with them the special and subjective meanings. For example, when the girl in the story was trying to paint, Nel was moving her fingers accordingly; when the girl's feelings of frustration and anger at the physicians was described Nel changed the expression of her face and the posture of her body, and asked for explanations of her own bodily experiences and remembered feelings. The conversations triggered by the book, the recalling, retelling and mutual searching of subjective and specific meaning were most important.

At the parent-dyad meetings both parents felt very moved, but much more confident. At the same time mother was able to confront father with her anger and disappointment with him and father was ready to listen to her. Nel was much easier to handle and there was a pleasant atmosphere at home in spite of a forthcoming forced change of living quarters and move to a new place that the family had to face.

It was mutually decided to conclude the treatment. Both parents felt that they understood and could respond to Nel's needs. Mother decided to work less and to spend more time taking care of her two children. Nel seemed to be a cheerful and well-adjusted girl, ready for new experiences and new relationships. In a follow-up conversation six months later, mother reported that Nel was very pleased with her teacher, had friends at school and seemed content and sure of herself.

Discussion

Mother, and consequently Nel, had relied excessively on splitting as a coping and defensive strategy, in an attempt to avoid frightening and painful feelings. The supportive and securely structured situation of dyadic treatment facilitated for Nel the integration of her self-understanding. The many possibilities for creative experiencing, the parents' participation in observing self and other, reciprocal influences and re-creation of significant experiences enhanced the child's developmental and integrative processes. The parents, especially the mother, were helped to differentiate between the child and themselves, and to mobilize the paternal and maternal resources needed for strengthening the child's self-righting tendencies and resilience.

Chapter 13

'The missing piece'

A dyadic treatment intended as a preparation for individual treatment of the child or simultaneous treatment of child and parents.

Therapist: A. Wasserman

The dyadic meetings with mother–child, father–child and mother–father lasted nine months with a frequency of two intermittent sessions a week. The simultaneous meetings of one session a week with the child and the parents lasted 14 months and ended with 3 months of mother–child and father–child dyadic meetings.

Alan, a 5-year-old boy, was referred by his parents because of extremely aggressive behaviour at home, where mother was the main victim of his assaults, and uncontrolled behaviour in nursery school, to the point that the children he assaulted sometimes needed medical care. Although a 'bully' he was liked and well esteemed by grown-ups as well as children in the nursery school. In the period prior to referral, Alan showed extreme fear of darkness, of monsters and snakes and had difficulty falling asleep. He complained of 'bad dreams' and would come up with sayings like 'I am a bad boy'. The parents refused to give him tranquillizers and asked for psychological help.

Alan is his parents' first and only child born after two natural miscarriages. The pregnancy was planned and welcomed but also accompanied by many anxiety-provoking medical procedures. Thanks to the gratifying experience of caring for the newborn baby, mother recovered quickly from a traumatic delivery.

Alan was described as a calm, easy-to-care-for baby, alert and curious, 'an interesting baby' in mother's words. From the age of six months he was taken care of by a nanny, as mother returned to work, and from one and a half years, he attended a day-care centre. According to the parents, Alan's 'behavioural problems' started at the age of 3 and gradually grew worse. Alan demonstrated severe distress without constant attention to his demands. He was extremely restless and easily threw temper tantrums, accompanied by hurling and breaking objects, and/or vomiting, the violence directed mainly at his mother. After such outbursts, mother would usually leave him alone for a while and then would soothe him. She described these moments as particularly important to her feeling very close to the child. Alan would sometimes, after an outburst, turn his picture, which hung on the wall above his bed, face down and say 'that's not me' or 'I don't want to see him any more'.

Mother complained about the cycles of Alan's rages which, like other acts of his, were 'completely incomprehensible' to her. He was described by both parents as a very gifted and intelligent child who calmed down mainly when intellectually stimulated by 'thinking games'. At the age of four, when he could already read fluently, he was transferred by his kindergarten teacher to a higher grade, but this did not appease the child's restlessness, anger and uncontrolled behaviour.

Mother described herself as exhausted with the constant need to control Alan, as the father was absent from home for many hours owing to his work. Father admitted that he was waiting for the boy to grow up to have 'discussions with him on physics, and so on' – subjects that interested the father. At present he felt bored and impatient with the 'childish' behaviour and interests of Alan.

Alan's mother, 30 years old at the time of the referral, had a senior position in an economic institute. The father, 34 years old, worked as an engineer in a hi-tech plant. Both considered themselves ambitious and professionally successful.

Mother, oldest of three children, had two brothers whom she perceived as a 'disturbing nuisance'. In the course of the therapy, it became known that her experience as a little girl was to have to grow up fast and always be considerate of her two 'younger' brothers. She described her relationship with her mother as permanently unsatisfactory – 'something was always missing'. She felt very dependent on her mother's approval, always wishing to be close to her but feeling rejected. Mother chose an occupation similar to her mother's and up to a late stage in therapy they both worked at the same institution.

Father was the youngest and only boy in his family. He remembers himself as 'not brilliant enough and not satisfying [his] ambitious father'.

Both parents saw themselves as a 'good couple and good parents'. They wished to have more children. They were genuinely worried and also angered by Alan's 'problems'. They related a natural miscarriage (the third one) six months ago as connected to their misgivings about raising Alan and the fear of having another boy like him.

The assessment process

(Two sessions with each parent–child dyad and two individual sessions with the child).

Alan, physically well developed for his age, is an easily likeable child. He gets very high marks on intelligence tests, expresses himself as a 'grown-up' and shows much interest and also good understanding of affective states of his own and of others.

In his play as well as in projective tests he was almost constantly preoccupied with themes of aggression that in his experience links and unites, but also frightens. He referred to himself as a destructive boy, insufficiently protected, and showed excessive anxiety regarding his body.

Alan seemed to be struggling but unable to separate from a 'togetherness' with the mother that was impeding his individuation. He drew his mother as a 'girl'. It was known from mother's report that he quite often complained to her 'why are you a girl, why aren't you a mother'?

Alan seemed easily annoyed when not related to according to his wishes. For example, when the therapist asked him to sit at a table he announced 'I am still small, I need a suitable chair' and claimed that the chair was too high for him. As soon as he was reassured that it was possible to adjust the chair to his size he calmed down.

In the interactions with mother, during the dyadic session, Alan mostly asked her to do things for him according to his choice, such as colouring a picture, while he would play a game with the therapist. To mother's reaction 'Why do you leave me alone? Why do you leave me out?', Alan insisted that she use the colour crayons he picked up, to which mother retorted that she 'also has the right to choose'.

A dialogue like one between peers competing for place, power and acceptance developed between mother and the child. Mother seemed hurt and rejected, Alan was distressed and anxious, apparently in conflict about giving in or staying on his own. Mother moved to belittle and even humiliate Alan, by fault-finding in the game he wanted to play with the therapist and in his choice of colours. She said: 'You are small, you don't known anything, what kind of colours have you chosen?' Despite mother's 'playful manner', Alan's anger was mounting and when he seemed on the edge of totally losing control mother went up to him (not before looking at the therapist as if to say 'you see what I mean') and hugged and pacified him. The session ended in a cuddly atmosphere of mother and Alan being together. As they went out of the room Alan said to his father, who was waiting for them, 'It was hard for Mom today, you must help her at home', then Alan turned to the therapist, repeating the question 'Do you have a husband?' which he had asked at the beginning of the session.

In the second dyadic session of mother and Alan the same pattern reappeared in their interaction: mother was in distress, feeling 'deserted' and unworthy when Alan showed more autonomy in expressing his needs and when he chose to be with someone else. Mother apparently needed Alan in a special way, to feel herself wanted, valued and efficient, as if only the child could supply her needs. She found it hard to integrate her role as Alan's mother and her 'girlish' sharing of his world. Alan tried to disentangle himself from the many special roles of companion, supplier, grown-up and child, but was unable to do it without help. It was quite obvious that he also found some fulfilment of his narcissistic needs in this kind of relationship.

In the dyadic sessions with his father, exactly as in the session with mother, Alan assigned him a picture of a dinosaur to colour. Father agreed to all his instructions and Alan happily announced 'There are good and bad dinosaurs; the good ones have bristles that are supposed to protect them from the bad ones. If the bristles fall off, new ones grow right away.' After a while, Alan suggested a make-believe war-play and 'shot' his father with a pistol, saying 'You are supposed to die now'. Father, looking angry and uncomfortable, retorted 'No. What kind of game is it anyway? Stop it immediately!' Appeased by the therapist, father agreed to participate in the game and 'came back to life'. Alan pleased, added: 'This is a game, you'll really die only when you are old.'

Father found it very difficult to engage in any pretend play situations with aggressive themes and to help Alan to distinguish between aggressive wishes and fantasies and anger-provoking experiences, in a secure enough atmosphere. It seemed that in similar play situations with mother and father, Alan poses both of them the same question: which one of us is the 'big' one and which one is 'small'?

Since the parents had difficulties in performing their parental roles without being aware enough of it as well as being genuinely anxious to help their child, a dyadic trial-learning period, as preparation for treatment, was suggested. The parents agreed easily and mother seemed even greatly relieved and pleased, although father expressed his concern that he might find it 'extremely boring'. The therapist was impressed by the force of Alan's conflicts about his dependence–independence needs and his low self-esteem, seemingly resulting from the incomprehensible, for him, parental as well as his own behaviour. The pervasive feeling of lack of other-regulation and inadequate self-regulation enhanced aggressive fantasies, and fear of retaliation.

Dyadic meeting with mother

Almost from the beginning Alan presented his parents with a question that seemed vital to him: who would take care of mother, whom he sensed was in need of help.

The following is an excerpt from a session which took place in the first month of treatment:

> Alan proudly shows the therapist a sweater his mother knitted for him. They start playing with different dolls. Alan is well attuned to his mother's wishes, and in fact lets her make the rules. When he expresses a wish of his own that changes the game she says, holding a clown doll in her hands: 'Do you know that clowns are in fact sad? They are happy only when children are around. As soon as the children go away, as soon as the audience leaves, they are sad and lonely'.
>
> Alan becomes increasingly upset and yells: 'No, no, no! Don't say that! They are not sad', but mother continues: 'Yes, they need an audience. They are sad without the children....' Alan is very upset and tense, on the verge of a tantrum.
>
> The therapist intervenes: 'The clowns can be sad and in need of help, but it is not the children's task to help them; they have to do children's stuff. Someone else can be found to help the clowns when it is difficult for them'.
>
> Mother agrees and so does Alan, who says to the therapist: 'Mother is crazy. I am mad at her', to which the therapist remarks: 'Mothers also find it difficult to always know and help their children, but other people can also help mothers'. 'No, I'm crazy', he answers. 'I'm mad at myself.' 'Children are occasionally so angry with their parents', says the therapist, 'that maybe it is scary, so they prefer to be angry with themselves'.

Alan is pacified and mother and child leave the consulting room hugging each other and appeased.

At a session one month later, Alan suggested that he and mother read once more *The Missing Piece*, a book he used to peruse at the beginning of each session. Alan was interested to reflect on unpleasant feelings and to discuss with mother 'how it feels', a question from the book.

> Therapist: 'Each one of us misses something, and we have different feelings about it.'

Alan suggests that they draw 'houses like people'. He draws a house with teeth, an angry house, and says: 'Nobody comes near him because he bites. The house hates the bad guys who did all sorts of things to him. So he doesn't let the good guys come in either.' The therapist elaborates on different possible feelings such as the need for protection, feelings of loneliness, etc.

In response Alan asks the therapist to draw a friend for the house and a fence. Then he asks mother to draw houses. She draws several houses, gives them facial expressions and writes down next to each one the emotion it expresses. Alan is pleased and participates in determining the titles. Mother wants to make an angry house and says: 'I can't do it. It doesn't come out right.' Alan tries to help her draw the house but does not succeed. The therapist suggests that Alan and mother should each draw an angry house, because everyone is angry in his own and different way. Mother: 'I can only manage to draw a weeping empty house instead of an angry one.' Eventually she succeeds in drawing an angry house, and says: 'I can only draw one with a moustache.' Alan continues to draw houses and mother pays attention to what he is doing, and gives them descriptive titles. She underscores his sad and angry houses. Each one writes next to his angry house what the house expresses. Alan says: 'My angry house sometimes feels so mad, but it doesn't even know why. It's puzzling, it's confusing.'

It was quite obvious that Alan sensed his mother's keen distress. He tried to function as her 'missing piece' and kept 'rescuing' her. In the process of therapy he started to feel reassured that someone else could replace him in this role.

Dyadic meeting with father

In his parallel sessions with father, Alan was preoccupied with the same problem he dealt with in the sessions with mother, i.e. who was responsible for taking care of mother.

Alan and father are engaged in a play with puppets. They discuss who will operate the father-bear and mother-bear and who will hold the small baby bear. Alan asked father to hold the grown-up bears, as he wants to hold the baby bear. Alan decides that mother-bear has a wound. Father caresses mother-bear and agrees that she has to be treated. The therapist: 'The baby bear asks who will take care of mother?', to which father answers: 'Perhaps father-bear'. Alan is pleased and says to father: 'You will never be a girl.'

Later in the session Alan takes a small teddy bear and caresses it, saying: 'You are cute. I'll take care of you.'

At a later session, Alan discussed with father whether children should sleep alone or with their parents. He also told him about 'mother-bear who feeds her cubs with food she knows they don't like because she needs to hear their complaints, it soothes her', probably alluding to his experiences with mother.

As it emerged in these sessions, Alan wished to free himself from the role of his mother's 'tranquillizer', yet he would not do it until there was someone to substitute him. Supported by the therapist's clarifications he was able to show father his needs from him and from mother.

Dyadic meeting with mother

Having 'found' a new caregiver for mother, Alan went one step further and expressed his wish to have a private corner of his own in the room, with mother's permission.

Alan speaks in a private language understandable to him only, and uses a secret writing – obviously in an attempt to separate himself. Mother reacts by being distressed, feeling deserted and betrayed. She demands to share his secrets.

When the different needs of Alan and mother are focused upon by the therapist and discussed in the sessions, Alan erects three walls in the room – to form three corners: one for himself, one for mother and one for the therapist.

He defines the boundaries of each corner and is dealing with various questions: When does one go from one's corner to someone else's corner; how does one ask permission to enter someone else's corner; how does one feel when one is alone in a corner; how does one feel when one wants to visit someone else in his corner, but the 'host' cannot receive 'guests' just then?

Both Alan and mother realize that they find it hard to be alone in their respective corners. Alan says: 'I don't understand what is happening in each corner, that's why I need many sessions to explore the subject of the corners.'

The therapist verbalizes and helps mother to relate empathically to the child's feelings and to grant legitimacy to wishes, without converting them immediately into actions. Supported and feeling understood, Alan and mother are listening to each other. They talk about their loneliness and sadness, without doing anything right away to eradicate the feeling. They 'explain' to each other how it feels to be angry, happy, worried. Mother recalled how it was when she was a little girl, and who comforted her and so on.

Mother's difficulty with being available to Alan in sad and frightening experiences was extremely frustrating to him. From mother's point of view such feelings in her child made her an inadequate mother, like the one she had. She was 'forcing' Alan to feel that only mother can help him to feel good. Mother's repeated intrusions into the child's feeling states were one of the reasons for Alan's rages. He was expected to accept that to separate and individuate was translated by mother as 'deserting her'.

Dyadic meeting with father

During the 'corner' period Alan fashioned corners in the sessions with his father too, but used them differently. He 'paired' father with the therapist and went to 'sleep' in his own corner. From time to time he would 'wake up' perturbed and tell about his fears. In the secure atmosphere of the therapeutic room, he was able to actualize many of his fantasies, anxieties and memories. He brought maimed dolls to the sessions and initiated situations in which the light in the therapeutic room was turned off, asking what happens at night in 'the grown-ups' bedroom'. Father, with some help from the therapist, responded in a supporting and containing manner to Alan's anxieties as well as his autonomy needs.

Further meeting with mother

The next important issue Alan examined in the sessions with mother was whether she would allow a new coalition of father and son in their family triangle.

Alan brought aeroplanes which he had assembled in the sessions with father, and showed mother how beautiful they were. He would not let her participate in their construction. Mother was hurt and angry with him, and verbalized her displeasure.

The therapist helped mother to look upon Alan's needs as developmentally normative, and encouraged her to think of every relationship as one of a kind. At the same time she was empathic with mother's disappointment and concern that her close relations with Alan might be spoiled if they were not exclusive.

Alan participated by describing the unique relations he had with mother, and mentioned things he did only with her, yet clearly expressed his wish for relations with father, even though mother did not take an active part in them.

Further meeting with father

Alan's relations with father were building up on the basis of their being men. It was father who introduced rivalry into their meetings: he cheated when he lost in games, was upset when Alan insisted on leading and deciding on subjects of play and was reluctant to participate in discussions about power, fitness or roughness as attributes of masculinity, although the boy challenged him to do this. The therapist supported father actively in his parental role by helping him to accept but also separate his childlike wishes and fantasies from the here-and-now reality of his parenthood. Soon, father and son were busily engaged in 'boys'' games for many sessions, assembling aeroplanes, having car races, even wrestling. The therapist's role was to set the scene for their 'male-only' interactions and togetherness.

Alan could talk about his feelings with father, and clarify whether they were proper for 'men'. At this stage of the therapy, when Alan 'killed' for example, father co-operated easily, and was able to enter the world of make-believe. When Alan expressed his castration anxiety, father was able to guide him to see the difference between imagination and reality. By forming an alliance with father, Alan's understanding of his 'role' as a boy was reinforced. As a result he was more relaxed and reassured in his separate and independent existence with mother too.

Meetings with the mother–father dyad

Parallel to the meetings of the parent–child dyads there were regular once-a-fortnight meetings with the parents, aimed at working through the themes and experiences of the dyadic sessions and the memories that they evoked.

The parents brought up spontaneously their unsatisfactory marital relations. Quite soon their claim that Alan was the obstacle to better relationships was replaced by the recognition that they placed him between them, both emotionally and physically, by gladly letting him sleep in bed with them.

Mother complained about father's absences from home for longer than she could bear ever since Alan was 2 years old. She was angry and disappointed but found it difficult to express her feelings of loneliness and distress.

Father had been alienated from his wife and child and had let it happen as a reaction to the hurt he felt.

The parents were encouraged to talk about the loneliness they felt, personally and socially, which they tried to alleviate by spending most of the time with Alan. The primary goal of the meetings was to enhance mother and father's parental abilities by gaining greater awareness of Alan's difficulties and learning more effective ways of dealing with them.

Mother began to 'decipher' the meaning of the 'vicious circle' she had entered in her relations with Alan. She realized that when Alan 'left' her, namely did not attend to her needs, she felt 'deserted' and 'left alone'. She could identify her reaction pattern, which she knew would enrage Alan and to which she resorted in times of distress. She shared with father and the therapist her memories when as a small girl she was not allowed by her mother to complain or be angry and had been led to accept that she was not entitled, even now, to express her negative feelings. Mother was able to see that Alan was actualizing different roles (unconsciously projected on him) and was anxiously attuned to her needs from him. Dependency and 'merging' needs, needs for approval, support and stable boundaries between self and other were discussed between and with the parents.

Father recognized his competitiveness and ambitions, and began to acknowledge the fantasies he had been afraid to encounter. As the therapy sessions progressed he came to understand better that the boredom he felt with Alan was a defence against his anxiety to face the 'child' in himself.

The parents became aware of the change that was talking place in Alan. Now he could more often distance himself from them both physically and emotionally, and return when he needed or missed them. His tantrums gradually decreased and were replaced by verbal 'corrections' on his part when his parents were not in tune with him.

At the end of this period it seemed that Alan, progressing faster than his parents, would benefit from individual sessions, with the parents continuing in simultaneous meetings with the same therapist, and working on the parallel events in Alan's and their treatment as his parents.

The middle phase – individual sessions with Alan

Alan started his first individual session by asking the therapist to play the games he used to play with mother, then the one he used to play with father and one his parents had taught him at home. The therapist understood this as his way of appeasing anxiety and preserving the parents' presence for him in the room, in a kind of dialogue that started during their common sessions. Quite unusually, both parents, during the whole period, were accompanying Alan to each session and waiting for him in an adjacent room.

Alan started the sessions by reading the books *The Missing Piece* and *The Fish who did not want to be a Fish*, proceeding to compose sequels to the stories.

The themes that he worked on consisted of questions about autonomy–dependence, differences and similarities, experiences of defeat and victory of being good or bad. He would elaborate with the therapist's help on his own and others' feelings, on the kind of relations he could safely have with his mother, father and with them as a married couple. He wanted to understand the various aspects in context of his self-representation and self-evaluation experiences as well as oedipal wishes and anxieties.

In this phase of the treatment he was mostly elaborating on fantasies deriving from sexual wishes. The more he dared to express his wishes the more he became aware of his castration anxieties: he wondered if a girl could become a boy.

He was frightened by his fantasy that the therapist needed something which he had (a missing piece), and that she would take it away from him, just as he was planning to take things from her.

He initiated situations in which he took off his clothes, to see what she would do to him.

He expressed pride in his army (in a war-game), praising it as big and beautiful, and wondered who would defend it from the therapist.

He asked whether she needed him as a girl so he would have to act as one and proposed that she take girls for therapy too, and they would play girls' games with her while he would play boys' games.

When Alan was no longer worried about a woman's envy he started to explore the possibility of a man punishing him for his wishes.

During the concluding session of this period, Alan played with the therapist the memory game he used to play with his parents. When he got to the snake he said: 'This is mine. It makes me happy, it is beautiful.' When he got to the angry lady he said: 'This one is yours. I'll take the angry man.' At the end of this session he announced happily: 'This fish likes to be a fish.'

In the parallel sessions with the parents, mother and father focused on their relations as Alan's parents. They greatly enjoyed the sharing during their regular 'waiting meetings' once a week when accompanying Alan to his therapy.

As their treatment progressed it became possible for mother to realize how many roles Alan played for her and instead of her. With the help of the therapist and her husband, mother was able to focus on her present adult wishes as a wife, as a mother, and to try to integrate into them her disavowed needs as a 'rejected girl'. Father learned to fulfil more adequately his role as a husband, as a supporting father to Alan and a 'second other' in the triadic relations.

The ending phase

The decision to end the therapy was concurrently reached by the parents, the therapist and Alan. All felt pleased with the progress and the changes that had been accomplished. It was decided to take about three months to work through the ending phase of the therapy.

In the following meeting Alan refused to enter the consulting room by himself. When asked what would make him come in he said that he wanted one of his parents to go in with him, 'so that we'll be three, not two'. The therapist's attempts to invite him alone increased his unease, and he burst into tears, saying: 'You really don't understand. I need my parents inside.'

This episode initiated a three-month period in which Alan 'reverted' to the original dyadic pattern with father or mother coming to the sessions intermittently, until the final parting.

Dyadic sessions with mother

In this series of sessions Alan, who had a more balanced relationship with mother, re-examined the subject of twosomes and threesomes, and mother's acceptance of his wish to be with someone else. Feeling secure in his sexual identity Alan checked with mother how she accepted the fact that he was a boy, and that there were things which were exclusively reserved for father. For instance, when he showed her once more how fast he could assemble an aeroplane, he was delighted that she expressed her admiration, and said: 'This is something I learned from Dad. I can assemble a plane better than both of you. I'm a boy.'

Mother and Alan discussed the changes in their dealings at home, and his growing capacity to have friends and new interests as well as behaving like a 'big boy'. They talked about parting from the therapist and being sad about it. Alan seemed to rely on mother's help and stated that he would need it when they stopped coming.

In the parting session mother and Alan were colouring a mosaic. Alan had a lion and mother an eagle to colour. Mother remarked: 'The lion is beautiful, but where is his tail?' Alan smiled triumphantly, as if saying 'So you did notice!', and coloured in the tail right away, commenting to the admiring mother: 'A lion without a tail is no lion at all.'

Dyadic sessions with father

Alan showed father how much he had grown and how he could now do things he had not be able to do the previous year.

Alan and father expressed their gratitude freely and their pleasure in the accomplishments during the therapy process, pointing out the many and new options that Alan had in reality to resort to.

Mother–father dyad

The parents called the therapist's attention to the fact that for the first time not all three of them came together. During the dyadic sessions of father with Alan, mother seized the opportunity to go out with her friends for 'ladies' pastimes', pleased that she could let them spend time together without her. She also felt proud that she had learned to enjoy the company of people of her own age and to take care of her own affairs.

She spoke of her wish to have another child – preferably a girl. She was sure that she was ready, feeling that her motherhood was now firmly established. She also spoke about her wish to obtain help for herself.

The parents acknowledged the great change that had taken place in their marital relations. They recognized the extent to which Alan had been mother's 'mate' and understood how his development was entangled and arrested. Father found in Alan a possible partner, whom he was no longer bored with, or impatiently waiting for to grow up.

In summary

There was now a definite distinction between the child's and the parents' roles as well as more satisfying dyadic mother–son and father–son relations. Both parents felt more confident in their parental role. In addition to the regret they felt as therapy was drawing to an end, they expressed their trust that the changes in their capacities as parents were not temporary.

Mother and Alan learned to define more accurately their expectations of each other, which enabled Alan to understand and disentangle, in a way, from his role of mother's caregiver.

He was given support and approval by his parents through the therapist, who reassured him that he was not disloyal or hurting mother when working through his needs and reflecting on his own and on the mental states of others. He attained enough security in his new and stable self-definition, his gender identity, as well as in his role in the family triangle that enabled new interactions and relations.

The therapist acted mostly as a translator and mediator, facilitating new understanding and protecting the child's and mother's feelings of separateness and self-differentiation. As a transference and real object the therapist validated the different interrelations, as well as an integration of relations with father as the 'second other'. The parents, more secure in their parental roles, helped Alan to integrate his wishes with realistic possibilities and the needs for acceptance with his self-expression.

References

Ackerman N (1966) Treating the Troubled Family. New York: Basic Books.

Basch MF (1992) Practising Psychotherapy. New York: Basic Books.

Belsky J, Pensky E (1988) Developmental history, personality and family relationships: Toward an emergent family system. In Hinde RA, Stevenson-Hinde J (Eds) Relationships within Families: Mutual Influences. Oxford: Oxford University Press, pp 193–217.

Ben-Aaron M, Avimeir-Patt R, Harel J, Kaplan H (1996) The mother–child and father–child psychotherapy. Paper presented at the Sixth World Congress of the World Association for Infant Mental Health, 25–28 July, Tampere, Finland.

Ben-Aaron M, Harel J (1997) The child's active role in the move from two to two plus one as seen in the mother–child and father–child psychotherapy – a dynamic approach to treatment of relational disturbances in childhood. Paper presented at the 21st Annual Conference of the Israeli Association of Psychotherapy, 22–24 May, Tiberias, Israel.

Ben-Aaron M, Harel J, Kaplan H, Patt R, Glat D, Raz E, Wasserman A, Winer M (1997) Mother–child and Father–child Psychotherapy: A Manual for the Treatment of Relational Disturbances in Childhood. Haifa: University of Haifa Department of Psychology (in Hebrew).

Bion WR (1962) A theory of thinking. International Journal of Pycho-Analysis 43: 306–310.

Bowen M (1978) Family Therapy in Clinical Practice. New York: Aronson.

Bowlby J (1979) The Making and Breaking of Affectional Bonds. London: Tavistock Publications.

Bowlby J (1980) Attachment and Loss, Vol. 3: Sadness and Depression. London: Hogarth Press and Institute of Psycho-Analysis.

Brazelton TB (1984) To Listen to a Child. New York: Addison-Wesley.

Brazelton TB (1992) Touchpoints. New York: Guilford Press.

Bretherton I (1987) New perspectives on attachments relationships: Security communication and internal working models. In Osofsky JD (Ed) Handbook of Infant Development. New York: Wiley, pp 1061–1100.

Byng-Hall J (1995) Rewriting Family Scripts: Improvisation and Systems Change. New York: Guilford Press.

Cicchetti D, Aber J (1986) Early precursors to later depression: an organizational perspective. In Lipsitt L, Rovee-Collier C (Eds) Advances in Infancy, Vol. 4. Norwood, NJ: Ablex pp 87–137.

Clarke-Stewart KA (1978) And daddy makes three: The father's impact on mother and young child. Child Development 49: 466–478.

Cramer B (1992) The Importance of Being Baby. New York: Addison-Wesley.

Cramer B, Robert-Tissot C, Stern DN, Serpa-Rusconi S, De Muralt H, Besson G, Palacio-Espasa E, Bachmann J, Knauer D, Berney C, D'Arcis U (1990) Outcome evaluation in brief mother–infant psychotherapy: a preliminary report. Infant Mental Health Journal 11: 278–300.

Dunn J, Plomin R (1991) Why are siblings so different? The significance of differences in sibling experiences within the family. Family Process 30: 271–284.

Emde RN (1988a) Development terminable and interminable, I: Innate and motivational factors from infancy. International Journal of Psycho-Analysis 69: 23–42 .

Emde RN (1988b) Development terminable and interminable, II: Recent psychoanalytic theory and therapeutic considerations. International Journal of Psycho-Analysis 69: 283–286.

Emde RN (1990) Mobilising fundamental modes of development: empathic availability and therapeutic action. Journal of the American Psychoanalytic Association 38: 881–913.

Emde RN (1991) The wonder of our complex enterprise: steps enabled by attachment and the effects of relationships on relationships. Infant Mental Health Journal 12: 164–173.

Fivaz-Depeursinge E, Stern D, Burgin D, Byng-Hall J, Corboz-Warnery A, Lamour M, Lebovici S (1994) The dynamics of interfaces: seven authors in search of encounters across levels of description of an event involving a mother, father and baby. Infant Mental Health Journal 15: 69–89.

Fonagy P (1994) Mental representations from an intergenerational cognitive science perspective. Infant Mental Health Journal 15: 57–68.

Fonagy P, Moran G (1991) Understanding psychic changes in child pychoanalysis. International Journal of Psycho-Analysis 72: 25–32.

Fonagy P, Steele M, Moran G, Steele H, Higgitt A (1993a) Measuring the ghost in the nursery: an empirical study of the relation between parents' mental representations of childhood experiences and their infants' security of attachment. Journal of the American Psychoanalytic Association 41: 957–89.

Fonagy P, Moran G, Edgcumbe R, Kennedy H, Target M (1993b) The roles of mental representations and mental processes in therapeutic action. Psychoanalytic Study of the Child 48: 9–47.

Fonagy P, Target M (1996a) A contemporary psychoanalytic perspective: psychodynamic developmental therapy. In Hibbs E, Jensen P (Eds) Psychosocial Treatment for Child and Adolescent Disorders: Empirically Based Strategies for Clinical Practice. Washington, DC: APA and NIH, pp 619–38.

Fonagy P, Target M (1996b) Playing with reality, I: Theory of mind and the normal development of psychic reality. International Journal of Psycho-Analysis 77: 217–33.

Fonagy P, Target M (1997) Attachment and reflective function: their role in self-organization. Development and Psychopathology 9: 679–700.

Fraiberg S, Adelson E, Shapiro V (1975) Ghosts in the nursery: a psychoanalytic approach to the problem of impaired infant–mother relationships. Journal of the American Academy of Child Psychiatry 14: 387–422.

Framo JL (1992) Family-of-Origin Therapy: An Intergenerational Approach. New York: Brunner/Mazel.

Freud A (1965) Normality and Pathology in Childhood. London: Hogarth Press.

Furman E (1992) Toddlers and Their Mothers. New York: International Universities Press.

Greenson RR (1967) The Technique and Practice of Psychoanalysis. New York: International Universities Press.

Gurman A, Kniskern D (Eds) (1981) Handbook of Family Therapy. New York: Brunner/Mazel.

Haley J (1984) Ordeal Therapy. New York: Jossey-Bass.

Hinde R (1979) Toward Understanding Relationships. New York: Academic Press.

Hoffman L (1981) Foundations of Family Therapy. New York: Basic Books.

Horowitz MJ (1988) Introduction to Psychodynamics: A New Synthesis. New York: Basic Books.

Hurry A (Ed)(1998) Psychoanalysis and Developmental Therapy. London: Karnac Books.

Kennedy H, Moran G (1991) Reflections on the aims of child psycho-analysis. Psychoanalytic Study of the Child 46: 181–98.

Kohut H (1977) The Restoration of the Self. New York: International Universities Press.

Kohut H (1984) How does Analysis Cure? Chicago: University of Chicago Press.

Lieberman AF, Pawl J (1993) Infant–parent psychotherapy. In Zeanah C (Ed) Handbook of Infant Mental Health. New York: Guilford Press, pp 427–42.

Mahler MS (1968) On Human Symbiosis and the Vicissitudes of Individuation. New York: International Universities Press.

Mahler MS, Pine F, Bergman A (1975) The Psychological Birth of the Human Infant. New York: Basic Books.

McDonough S (1993) Interaction guidance: understanding and treating early infant–caregiver relationship disorders. In Zeanah C (Ed) Handbook of Infant Mental Health. New York: Guilford Press, pp 414–26.

Minuchin S (1974) Families and Family Therapy. Cambridge, MA: Harvard University Press.

Minuchin S, Fishman C (1981) Family Therapy Techniques. Cambridge, MA: Harvard University Press.

Moran GS (1987) Some functions of play and playfulness: a developmental perspective. Psychoanalytic Study of the Child 42: 11–29.

Muir E (1992) Watch, wait and wonder. Infant Mental Health Journal 13: 319–28.

Palazzoli-Selvini M, Bosolo L, Cecchin C, Prata O (1978) Paradox and Counterparadox. New York: Aronson.

Papousek H, Papousek M (1979) Early ontogeny of human social interaction. In von Cranach M, Foppa K, Lepenies W, Ploog D (Eds) Human Ethnology: Claims and Limits of a New Discipline. Cambridge: Cambridge University Press.

Patterson GR (1980) Coercive Family Processes. Eugene, OR: Castalia.

Pedersen FA (Ed) (1980) The Father–Infant Relationship. New York: Praeger.

Plomin R, Daniels D (1987) Why are children in the same family so different from one another? Behavioural and Brain Sciences 10: 1–16.

Reisman J, Ribordy S (1993) Principles of Psychotherapy with Children. Lexington, MA: Lexington Books.

Rolf J, Mosten AS, Cicchetti D, Neuchterlein KH, Weintraub S (Eds) (1990) Risk and Protective Factors in the Development of Psychopathology. Cambridge: Cambridge University Press.

Sandler J (1976) Countertransference and role-responsiveness. International Review of Psychoanalysis 3: 43–7.

Sandler J (1990) Internal objects and internal object relationships. Psychoanalytic Inquiry 10: 163–81.

Sandler J (1994) Fantasy defence and the representational world. Infant Mental Health Journal 15: 26–35.

Sandler J, Kennedy H, Tyson R (1980) The Technique of Child Psychoanalysis. London: Hogarth Press.

Sandler J, Sandler A-M (1978) On the development of object relationships and affects. Journal of Psycho-Analysis 59: 285–96.

Sandler J, Sandler A-M (1992) Psychoanalytic technique and theory of psychic change. Bulletin of the Anna Freud Centre 15: 35–51.

Sandler J, Sandler A-M (1997) A psychoanalytic theory of repression and the unconscious. In Sandler J, Fonagy P (Eds) Recovered Memories of Abuse: True or False? London: Karnac Books, pp 163–81.

Satir V (1967) Conjoint Family Therapy. New York: Science and Behaviour Books.

Sholevar G, Burland J, Frank J, Etezady M, Goldsein J (1989) Psychoanalytic treatment of children and adolescents. Journal of the American Academy of Child and Adolescent Psychiatry 28.

Slipp S (1993) The Technique and Practice of Object Relations Family Therapy. New York: Jason Aronson.

Stern DN (1985) The Interpersonal World of the Infant. New York: Basic Books.

Stern DN (1991) Maternal representations: a clinical and subjective phenomenological view. Infant Mental Health Journal 12: 174–86.

Stern DN (1994) One way to build a clinically relevant baby. Infant Mental Health Journal 15: 36–54.

Sullivan HS (1953) The Interpersonal Theory of Psychiatry. New York: Norton.

Target M, Fonagy P (1996) Playing with reality, II: The development of psychic reality from a theoretical perspective. International Journal of Psychoanalysis 77: 459–79.

Vygotsky LS (1978) Mind in Society. Cambridge, MA: Harvard University Press.

Wachtel E, Wachtel P (1986) Family Dynamics in Individual Psychotherapy. New York: Guilford Press.

Watzlawick P, Weakland J, Fisch R (1974) Change: Principles of Problem Formation and Problem Resolution. New York: Norton.

Whitaker C, Napier A (1978) The Family Crucible. New York: Harper & Row.

Winnicott DW (1965) The Maturational Processes and the Facilitating Environment. New York: International Universities Press.

Winnicott DW (1971) Therapeutic Consultations in Child Psychiatry. New York: Basic Books.

Winnicott DW (1982) Playing and Reality. Harmondsworth: Penguin Books.

Index

Printed and bound by CPI Group (UK) Ltd, Croydon, CR0 4YY

13/09/2026

14961033-0001